The Cittie of **Bristoll** standeth upon ÿ borders of Somersett & Gloucester [...] Cittie & Countie of it self: It's Scituation is in a pleasant Vale upon ÿ two R[...] is much the Lesser river yet on it standeth the Cheif Key of this Cittie [...] spring tide neere 40 foot in height bringing up thither shipps of great bu[...] about three miles downe the river and are for the most part discharged by lighters. Iust below this Cittie the river Froom falleth into the river Avon. which about Six miles lower falleth into the great River Seaverne but by the way hath a wonderfull passage through a mighty hill leaveing on each side very high & stupendious Rocks. that on the North side is called St Vincents rock. where are found those adamantine like stones or Bristoll-Diamonds. which are famous in most parts of Europe & elswhere. & which (as Cambden affirmeth) only in point of hardness come short of ÿ Diamonds of India: On ÿ top of this rock are seene ÿ footsteps of some larg but very antient fortification. And out of ÿ bottom thereof issueth a famous medicinall warme Bath water. comonly called ÿ Hotwell. much frequented at all convenient seasons of ÿ yeare. both by ÿ neighbouring Cittisens & also by Others. who liueing farr remote. resort thither for health sake. This Cittie is governed by A Maijor. 12 Aldermen. two shrieffs & a Common Councill. consisting in all of ÿ number of 48: Vsually once every yeare there is held a generall Sessions of ÿ peace. & Court of Oyer & Terminer. before ÿ Right worshipfull the Maijor. ÿ Recorder. & Court of Aldermen for delivering of ÿ Goale. & for inquirie into ÿ dammages of ÿ Crown. Towards ÿ East end of this Cittie former-ly stood a very larg & strong Castle. which since ÿ late Warrs hath bin demollished & is now turned into faire streets & pleasant dwellings. retaining still ÿ name of ÿ Castle. At ÿ West end of ÿ Cittie standeth ÿ Cathedrall Church & Bishops seat. in a most pleasant & wholesome aire neere where-unto are to be seene ÿ remaynes of Antient Cloysters. & other Religious houses. which in ÿ time of ÿ Warrs of England were defaced. & for ÿ most part ruined & since Continues in ÿ same condition. This Cittie sheweth 19 faire Churches whereof 17 are Parochiall. the chief-est of which standeth on ÿ south side of ÿ Cittie without ÿ Walles. which from ÿ Red. rock whereon it is founded is called St Marie Redcliff. which by reason of it's Stately scituation (being asscended vnto on ÿ Cittie-side by aboue 30 steps of stone) it's Archie foundation. heigth strength & largness of building. both for Chappell. Church & Tower. it's cross shape, & loftie Isles. it's beautifull porches. pinnacles battlements. & other Ornaments ÿ ren=ders it admireable. is held & deemed to be in all respects ÿ fairest parochiall Church in England. by reason. whereof it is highly esteemed by ÿ inhabitants & much admired by Strangers. It is wholely built of Free-stone without the Concurrance of any timber. either to ÿ structure or tecture of ÿ same. except a frame ÿ bears ÿ lead. Over ÿ River Avon passeth a very faire & loftie stone Bridg. built on either side with houses & shopps. wch though in length it cometh much short of. yet in fairnesse of buildings goeth as much beyond ÿ famous Bridg of London over Thames. There are no sincks ÿ come from any houses into ÿ streets. but all is conveyed vnder ground rendering ÿ Cittie exceeding sweet & delightsom. They vse no Carts there as in London. but carry all uppon Sledds: In few yeares last past this Cittie hath bin much augmented by ÿ increase of new buildings in most parts thereof especially on ÿ West & North west sides. where ÿ riseing of ÿ Hill St Michael being con-verted into Comely buildings & pleasant gardens makes a very beautifull addition to the suburbs thereof it is a place of verie great trade & Merchandize sending forth shipps into all parts of ÿ World. where trade=ing is allowed. In which respect as also for its number of inhabitants. and good Government. it may well be accounted One of ÿ cheiff Cities of this Kingdome. It is so pleasant to ÿ Eye. & so well accomodated with all things necessarie for life. or delight. so well furnished with plentifull Marketts. wholesome waters faire buildings Schooles. Hospitalls. & what ever else may be desired. that it well answers to its antient Saxon name. Brightstop. Signifying in English A most illustrious place: It hath been formerly dignified with the Honourable title of an Earldome. which the truely Noble familie of the Digbyes now enjoy. 1673.

Lectori. Otia quod vellent. quod vellet somnus habere
    Temporis. hic fructus. Candide Lector. habes
 Doctior. Autorem. culpando parcior esto,
    Accipiens facili mente. benignus. opus.

Quo. mihi cura fuit. revirescat ut inclitus. Urbis
    Splendor. et insignis. fiat. avitus honos.
 Æri commissæ. sit fama perennior ære.
    Urbis. et in to to nitior. Orbe. precor. IM

BRISTOL

A Pictorial History

Bristol Bridge, Jacob Millerd's map, 1673

BRISTOL

A Pictorial History

Donald Jones

Phillimore

1991

Published by
PHILLIMORE & CO. LTD.
Shopwyke Hall, Chichester, Sussex

ISBN 0 85033 780 1

Printed and bound in Great Britain by
BIDDLES LTD.,
Guildford, Surrey

List of Illustrations

Frontispiece: Bristol Bridge, Millerd's map, 1673

Illustration Acknowledgements

The author would like to thank the following individuals and institutions who loaned photographs and gave permission for their publication in this book: Bristol Record Office, 4, 14, 16-18, 22, 25, 28, 33, 42-46, 63, 66, 75, 83, 91, 93, 111, 113, 117, 125, 135, 137, 141, 162, 165, 167-171; Bristol Reference Library, 3, 49-51, 60, 73, 76, 79-81, 84, 92, 104, 124, 164, 174; Bristol United Press Ltd., 30-32, 146; City of Bristol Museum and Art Gallery, and the Industrial Museum, 6, 29, 47, 48, 52, 55, 68, 71, 78, 85, 86, 89, 94-97, 101, 105, 107, 108, 110, 119, 132, 134, 143, 144, 147, 148, 156, 158-161, 166, 172, 173, 175; Peter G. Davey Photograph Collection, 53, 54, 56, 58, 116, 139, 140, 145; Michael Farr, 69: map from E. J. Farr, A. T. G. Bower and R. M. Parsons, *Bristol City Docks Remembered, 1900-1973* (1986); Port of Bristol Authority, 74, 99, 100, 149-155, 157; Peggy Stembridge, 129.

Illustrations from J. F. Nicholls and J. Taylor, *Bristol Past and Present* Vols. I-III (1881) 5, 10, 11, 19, 70, 72; William Barrett, *The History and Antiquities of the City of Bristol* (1789) 12, 62.

Maps: William Smith (1568); John Speed (1610); Jacob Millerd (1673); John Feltham (1803); George Ashmead (1828).

Other photographs are from the author's own collection.

Introduction

W. H. Fox Talbot's famous photographic negative of his oriel window at Lacock Abbey was published in January 1839. When Daguerre published his discovery in March of the same year the art of photography was born. Before the advent of the photograph, however, no English city had a more extensive record of its early 19th-century appearance than Bristol. This was due to the retired merchant and West Indies plantation owner George W. Braikenridge, who between 1818 and 1830 commissioned and bought nearly 1,500 paintings and drawings of Bristol. This collection is now in the City Museum and Art Gallery. A local school of artists, led by Francis Danby and his friends Samuel Jackson and James Johnson, and including T. L. S. Rowbotham, H. B. O'Neill, W. J. Muller and J. B. Payne, created an attractive and intimate portrait of the city. They were not making souvenir paintings but responding in art to the city and ships they loved. The great Bristol photographers of the 19th century did no less.

Among the most remarkable of these men was Hugh Owen, the chief cashier of the G.W.R. in Bristol. Some of his evocative and sensitive work has survived in the Ellison Fuller-Eberle album (Ref. 28049[34]) at the Bristol Record Office. Others included J. B. Hazard, Fred Little, John Garratt, Edward Stevens and the professional, John York, whose collection survives in the City Museum. York took countless photographs of boats as they arrived at the mouth of the river and before they moored near his office on Broad Quay. The Central Reference Library has over 5,000 local photographs as well as a slide collection. The City Museum and the Industrial Museum have many thousands of photographs of industries, air, road and rail transport, in addition to John York's 2,000 ships. The City Record Office has a smaller but uniquely important archive, and a number of individuals have amassed vast collections. Among these Reece Winston's collection is internationally famous and has been published in many volumes over the years. Michael Tozer has specialised in transport and claims to have over 50,000 photographs, and Peter G. Davey's collection of trams and buses is very comprehensive. The Port of Bristol Authority, the Bristol United Press Library, Harveys of Bristol, Cadbury-Schweppes, British Aerospace, the Imperial Group, Stothert and Pitt Ltd., Dickinson-Robinson, and the University, all have pictorial archives.

With such an array of visual source material available no pictorial history can claim to be definitive, nor can any local historian expect to view it all. The businessmen who produced most of the photographs and postcards were not in business for the purpose of providing an historical record. They chose views they believed would sell. Many aspects of life have been completely ignored, but what they produced is of great value. This book is not an architectural, nor an industrial or business history. It is a visual record of change in a city, put into context and given structure by a brief historical commentary. The air raids on Bristol in the Second World War, and in particular the six major attacks which destroyed much of the old city, have made this visual record even more valuable.

Bristol, Seaport City

Bristol is an historic seaport city. Through the centuries it has maintained a strong sense of identity as a borough, and a county, with its own laws and customs which were proudly recorded in the *Mayor's Calendar* by the medieval town clerk, Robert Ricart. A long series of royal charters confirmed these rights and bestowed additional privileges, securing Bristol's future as a major city with a heritage richer than most. Bristol owes its prosperity and growth over the centuries to the exceptional drive of a number of individuals, Robert Sturmy, Canynges, Cabot, William Penn, Ferdinando Gorges, Brunel, and Sir George White, who were all outward-looking to a marked degree. The activities of its merchants, bankers, traders and industrialists, have fostered the city's growth from a medieval population of less than 15,000 to today's 390,000. Greater Bristol from Kingswood to Avonmouth, or from Filton to Dundry would include 600,000 people.

Approaching the city from any direction, one is aware that Bristol is not a conurbation, and, thanks to the green belt policy and to the agricultural economy of the west country, the city enjoys a rural hinterland. Based on a coalfield, and in the 19th century the focus of a railway network, Bristol's essential characteristics derive from its port and trade connections over the centuries. No one industry came to dominate this city, and it was never to experience industrial growth on the grand scale as seen in the Midlands and the North.

There was no Roman Bristol, since by the end of the first century the region already contained two tribal capitals, Cirencester and Caerwent, one legionary fortress, Caerleon, one military colony for retired legionaries, Gloucester, and a spa town, Bath. There was a Roman naval support base and small fort at Sea Mills, and there were several villas, but no town. Bristol's origins are Saxon. A passage in the *Anglo-Saxon Chronicle* for 1067 uses 'burh' when referring to Bristol, but in Alfred's scheme for the defence of Wessex against the Danes, Bristol is not listed among the important boroughs. The earliest reference to Bristol in the *Chronicle* reveals Bristol as a significant port and point of departure to Dublin in 1051. A seven-foot-high sculptured slab, dated *c.*1050, which was discovered serving as a coffin lid, and depicting Christ harrowing hell, lay long hidden beneath the floor of the Cathedral chapter house. This is the most dramatic evidence of the pre-Conquest Church to be seen in the city. Three pennies of Aethelred II (978-1016) struck at Bristol by the moneyer Aelfwerd, and presumably paid as Danegeld, are at Stockholm museum. A silver penny of Cnut, struck at Bristol by Aegelwine, can be viewed at the Ashmolean museum at Oxford. A mint implies a local demand for coinage and the existence of trade, so from the archaeological evidence we can postulate a thriving town.

Bristol was the 'Bricgstow' or 'place of the bridge' to Anglo-Saxon writers. It provided a crossing place at the confluence of two rivers, the Frome and the Avon, six miles inland from the sea, with good anchorage for ships. It was sited in a defensible position on three low hills rising 50 ft. above the marshes. The hill between the Avon and Frome provided the site for the castle and town; the second hill, west of the Frome, was chosen as the site of the monastery in 1140; the third hill, to the south, became the centre of the Redcliffe development. Cut off from much of the rest of the country by the great forests of Kingswood and Horwood north of the river, and by the forest of Bedminster south of the river, Bristol developed through the obvious way open to it, the sea. From the second greatest tidal rise and fall in the world, twice in every 24 hours, millions of tons of water push up the Gorge. Under the Suspension Bridge which now spans the Gorge 245 ft. above the Portway, the tidal range is 37 ft., while at the mouth where the Avon joins the Severn it is 41 ft.

So significant had the port of Bristol become by the time the anonymous Domesday surveyors arrived in 1086 that it was recorded as paying annually 110 marks of silver to the king, higher than that paid by any other town except London, York, Lincoln and Norwich. In addition to that sum the burgesses paid annually another 33 marks of silver, and one of gold, to Bishop Geoffrey of Coutances who was the effective viceroy for William I at Bristol. It must be said however that the Domesday commissioners did not distinguish clearly between the port and the large manor of Barton Regis of which Bristol was an appendage.

Bishop Geoffrey's first keep, built before 1088, was replaced from 1110 by Robert of Caen's castle which extended over 11 acres and was one of the strongest in the country. Robert, a natural son of Henry I, had been created Earl of Gloucester, and was the most powerful magnate in the area. He was half-brother to the Empress Matilda, and, during the civil wars of King Stephen's reign, 1135-54, Bristol Castle was the headquarters of her forces. King Stephen in 1141, Princess Eleanor for the whole of her life, and the unfortunate Edward II in 1327, were all imprisoned in the castle. Robert of Caen also founded in 1160, on an open site across the Frome, St James' Priory. Its nave has survived since 1374 as the parish church. He also sold a site on one of the three hills to Robert Fitzharding, the future Lord Berkeley, friend of the young king Henry II. Here, in 1140, Fitzharding founded the Abbey of St Augustine, and the Chapter House (c.1160) is widely considered to be England's finest Romanesque building of its kind.

Whereas the port's prosperity in the 11th and 12th centuries had been based on trade with Ireland, in 1152 Henry II had married Eleanor of Aquitaine, opening up the whole of her duchy, including Gascony, to trade. Every port in England imported some wine, but Bristol and Hull were the chief provincial centres for the wine trade. After wine, woad, used for dyeing cloth, is the most frequently-mentioned import in 13th-century records. Wool exports, which played such a prominent part in the trade of most English ports, were never of real significance at Bristol, although it was a Staple town. Cloth, on the other hand, was the basis of the city's trade and, while Italian or German merchants dominated the trade of many another English port, Bristol's merchants' influence here was paramount. It was a major harbour improvement in the 13th century that led to Bristol and Redcliffe's rapid expansion. This was the first of the two major civil engineering projects Bristol undertook in its history.

With a population of little more than 5,000, the townsmen in the early years of Henry III's reign began digging a massive trench across St Augustine's Marsh, some 2,400 ft. long, 18 ft. deep and 120 ft. wide. It took seven years, and, at the king's command, the men of Redcliffe were ordered to assist this project to cut a new channel for the Frome, and to build stone-faced quays on the town side. Expensive changes had been forced on the city because Bristol's first quay on the Avon could not cope with the pressure of shipping, and boats were left stranded for several tides on the stony river bed, straining their timbers. The city aimed to win back some of the shipping then going to Redcliffe

Back, hence the reluctance of the men of Redcliffe to help, and the intervention of the King. The new channel did much to establish the prosperity of the port in the following centuries as the ships could now rest on 'soft and oozy mud', and the new harbour was spacious.

When the Broad Quay was finished the townsmen set about replacing Bristol Bridge and building a new stretch of wall to fortify the town. To sink the three new piers the river had to be diverted, so a temporary channel was cut across from Tower Harritz, near Temple Meads, to Redcliffe Back. This ditch protected the new wall, built to enclose nearly all the area on the Somerset side of the Avon, but leaving Redcliffe Hill outside it. On the new bridge a double row of half-timbered houses grew up, as on London bridge. This bridge lasted until 1768 and its foundations are still there.

During the 14th century, war with France became a way of life, and Edward III in 1373, desperately short of money with which to continue the fighting, granted Bristol a charter, on payment of 600 marks, and also made it an independent county, giving it boundaries which included the Bristol Channel as far as the islands of Steep Holm and Flat Holm. The period of the charter, and of the new county status, saw also a remarkable flowering of originality in architecture. The High Cross was erected in 1373, to commemorate the charter, at the intersection of High Street, Wynch Street, Broad Street and Corn Street. It can now be seen at Stourhead, Wiltshire (on the National Trust property). The choir of St Augustine's Abbey had been built in the 1330s as a 'hall church', and the three vaulted aisles of equal height, with transverse beams withstanding the thrust of the main vault, created a great feeling of space. The almost complete replacement of the early St Mary Redcliffe commenced about 1340. In 1376 rebuilding was resumed from the transepts downwards, and by 1400 the whole nave may have been completed to create what Queen Elizabeth I believed to be the finest of English parish churches.

The Knights Templars had been continually in conflict with the city because of their independent rights of jurisdiction over the inhabitants who lived in the area of 'Temple Fee'. These rights included exemption from local taxation and providing sanctuary for criminals. In 1307 the king confiscated their lands and sold their property to the Knights of St John who began to build the present Temple church. The tower was commenced in 1398, but was built on soft, alluvial soil and tilted. Also at the end of the 14th century, the church of St John on the Wall was wholly rebuilt, without side aisles because of the narrowness of its site. By the close of the 14th century Bristol had grown far beyond the first city walls. Across the bridge over the Avon an industrial suburb had developed to the south where many cloth workers lived. The cloth workers, who had come to the 'Temple Fee' area under the patronage of the Knights Templars, had left Abbeville in Normandy where they had lived by the river Toque. The area of Bristol where they settled was called Touker Street in consequence, later to become Tucker Street. A 'tucker' was one who processed (shrank or fulled) newly woven cloth and hung it on 'tenters' to dry. A weavers' chapel was built on to Temple Church and a weavers' hall was established in Temple Street. One of the wealthier weavers, Edward Blanket, who lived in Tucker Street, became one of Bristol's M.P.s in 1362.

This was an age of faith when wealthy Bristol merchants showed a great desire to be benefactors. They believed they could reduce the time spent in Purgatory, after their death, by almsgiving to the poor, founding chantries where their souls could be prayed for, and endowing religious houses. John Barstable, for example, in 1395 founded the Trinity Almshouses in Old Market, and many families contributed to the building of St Mary Redcliffe, including William Canynges the younger. By the 15th century, Bristol merchants had endowed and supported many chantries, religious houses, hospitals and churches. Eighteen parish churches were packed inside the city walls, and the importance of the port is seen by the fact that the Dominicans, Franciscans, Carmelites and Augustinians all had religious houses round the town.

Bristol was by the 15th century already one of the three most important towns of England after London and York. But in terms of Europe it was still a small town and could not compare with the great cloth centres of the Low Countries. It was no Antwerp or Bruges, but it was well placed for a great future, and from the 15th century the port was the point of departure for numerous voyages of discovery. Bristol's seamen were already acquainted with the eastern shores of the Atlantic from Iceland to Gibraltar, and they were among the first to venture across the ocean. Like York and London, Bristol had its 'Fellowship of Merchant Adventurers' in the 15th century. They were mentioned in a petition to the Common Council in 1477 about the parlous state of the trade in Toulouse woad, and in 1500 detailed statutes were drawn up for the 'Company or Fellowship of the Marchauntes'. This reveals the merchants as exporting cloths each 'atte his adventure' to France, Portugal and Spain, and to Ireland and Iceland. The fortunes of the Gascon trade inevitably became closely involved with the Hundred Years War, and particularly when Bordeaux capitulated to France in 1451, followed by Bayonne in 1453. Although the trade made a recovery after 1475, imports of wine never again reached their pre-war level.

European voyages of discovery heralded a new era. In the late 15th century, following the fall of Constantinople in 1453, there commenced a series of voyages based on Portugal, to find a sea passage to southern Asia in the hope of opening direct trade for the spices that were now severely restricted. Another series of voyages, based largely on Spain, were made by a western or south-western route. To reach the Pacific they had to circumvent a huge land mass that they initially believed to be Asia, but which, by the 1520s, they came to accept was a New World. In 1493, the Spanish pope, Alexander VI, in a papal bull, later ratified as the Treaty of Tordesillas, 1494, divided the New World between Spain and Portugal. The treaty was never accepted by the other Atlantic states. Similarly, the profitability of trade with Africa first came to the attention of Bristol merchants through their ties with Portuguese traders in the 15th century. These Portuguese merchants were determined to preserve their lucrative business in slaves and to prevent other countries benefiting from it. Their protests to the English Crown led to a royal decree prohibiting merchants from taking part in the trade. Nevertheless Bristol merchants' long association with the Gold Coast began in 1552 when Sir Thomas Wyndham sailed from the port with three heavily-laden ships. A few years later William Hawkins was the first Bristol trader to carry slaves from Africa to the New World.

To Bristol belongs not only the discovery of Newfoundland but the credit for much of the pioneering work which led to the establishment of colonies in America in the 17th century. Some Bristol merchants, like John Jay in 1480, had set out to find the Island of Brazil, and John Cabot sailed in the *Matthew* in 1497, finding Newfoundland, which he thought was the Indies. Up to 28 boats left Bristol over the next seven years for the purposes of exploration. In 1509 Cabot's son, Sebastian, sailed from Bristol with two ships to investigate the North West Passage, but the city played no further part in the northerly passage ventures of his later years. These voyages were followed by those of Frobisher, Pring, Guy, Barker and Thomas James. As a result of their endeavours there followed the colonisation of the 17th century. This was due to the expenditure by private adventurers of great sums of money, backed by the herculean labours of the early colonists. For example, Sir Ferdinando Gorges, in the cause of plantations, is believed to have spent over £50,000 of his own money.

The Reformation in England had brought about momentous changes for Bristol. The skyline had been dominated by the abbey of the Augustinian Canons, the buildings of the White Friars near the site of Colston Hall, the Grey Friars in Lewin's Mead, the Dominican Friars in Broadmead, and the Austin Friars near Temple Gate. All these institutions were suppressed, releasing from Church control land for suburban development. Bristol also became a cathedral city in 1542, thus continuing in use the abbey of St Augustine. The Reformation also broke the Temple Fee and incorporated the area into the city of Bristol, thus ending the friction concerning the Redcliffe and Temple areas.

During the Civil War Bristol was besieged twice because it was considered by both sides to be of the utmost importance to their cause. On 9 December 1642 parliamentary forces managed to occupy the city, although Bristol had tried to remain uncommitted on both religious and political matters as long as it could. In July 1643 Prince Rupert's forces recaptured the town at the cost of 500 royalist lives. For the next two years Bristolians were subject to penal taxation and to forced labour in building three miles of fortified walls to the north of the city. The cost was enormous, but the value negligible, and Bristol surrendered to the Parliamentary forces under Fairfax, after a siege of only two weeks, in August 1654. Through constant tax burdens, uncleared filth, the spread of plague and the strain of billetting troops, the population of Bristol was reduced to desperate straits at the end of the year. It was followed by a long period of persecution of Dissenters and civic strife. Nevertheless, in trade and commerce Bristol slowly overtook Norwich as the second city of England.

Bristol was a major embarkation port for the colonies in the early 17th century, particularly to Virginia, New England and the West Indies. The majority of Bristol's emigrants were poor and undistinguished and probably most left as bonded servants. Others included political and religious offenders, kidnapped children, Civil War captives, and from 1718 common felons. For 30 years after 1654 every legally-bound servant who left Bristol was entered in a book, *Servants to Foreign Plantations*. This records the place of origin, occupation, age, sex, name, master, and the name of the colony to which the bonded servant was destined. This enrolment largely stopped when the negro began to replace the white man as the normal field worker on the tobacco and sugar plantations. However, indentured servants were still recorded as leaving through Bristol up to the American War of Independence, and during the years 1749-75, 3,279 servants went to Virginia and 707 to Maryland. It is not surprising therefore that Massachusetts and Rhode Island have counties named Bristol, and that there are at least 21 'Bristols' in America.

Bristol had particularly close connections with Pennsylvania. Admiral William Penn had been sent out by Cromwell in 1654 to capture Hispaniola from Spain. He failed to do this, but seized Jamaica instead. This turned out to be of great importance to England's position in the Caribbean, becoming the centre of the English slave trade in the area. It was not only a major sugar island but Kingston was the safest and most easily defended harbour in the British West Indies. The Admiral is buried in St Mary Redcliffe and some of his armour and ships' pennants are on the wall. In 1681 Charles II settled debts he owed to Admiral Penn by granting 47,000 square miles of territory in America to William Penn junior, whose second wife, Hannah Callowhill, was a Bristol girl. They were married in 1696 in Quakers Friars, Broadmead. Whilst in the city, Penn took as his secretary the schoolmaster at Quakers Friars from 1694, James Logan. Logan served in many offices in the new colony, becoming Chief Justice, and Governor.

By 1700 Bristol had reached the dawn of its golden age. In the next 130 years its population trebled, the old city was largely rebuilt and extensive new growth occurred along the riverside as the development of Lower Clifton and the Hotwells took place. The largely medieval areas such as the parishes of Temple, Redcliffe and St Thomas were left untouched. The manufacture of glass, pottery, brass, sugar-refining, brewing, soap-making, tobacco-refining, lead-smelting, and the more traditional dockside occupations, came to be increasingly important.

Bristol was the first of the outports to show a regular interest in the slave traffic when the Royal Africa Company's monopoly was ended in 1698, and as a result has attracted much obloquy. Between 1728-32, 48 ships a year were sailing from Bristol for slaves, but, even at this time of maximum involvement, this did not represent more than 12 per cent of the city's annual ship clearances. David Richardson's researches have revealed 2,108 Bristol slave ventures from 1698-1807, averaging 20 ventures a year, with more than 250 slaves each. From 1738, Liverpool and London's clearances passed those of Bristol. Of the 2.8 million slaves carried by English ships, Bristol accounted for a fifth, and a List of the Company of Merchants trading to Africa, required by Act of Parliament in June 1759, showed 241 Bristol merchants involved at that time.

Such merchants as Isaac Hobhouse, Onesiphorus Tyndall, Richard Farr, and Abraham Isaac Elton, shipped gin and copper to Africa, embarked slaves and transported them to the West Indies and America, sold them, and returned with cargoes of raw cotton, sugar, molasses and tobacco. Profits on a single voyage could be as high as £7-8,000, but perhaps one third of slave voyages failed to yield any profits at all. This might be due to hurricanes and shipwreck, wartime seizure, deaths among the slaves of up to 15-20 per cent on the crossing, and the ravages of the Toredo worms on the ships' timbers. Bristol merchants made far greater profits from privateering in time of war than from slaving. Most only risked a portion of their capital in slave ventures, being involved in sugar-refining, banking, the brass and copper industries, and in trading elsewhere besides Africa. Merchants were usually involved for only a limited period and were trading partners in African ventures alongside several others, while 120 organising agents managed only one voyage each. The golden age of Bristol's trade did not rest on trade to Africa, and by the time of the American War of Independence Bristol's share was down to 10 per cent. When abolition of the slave trade came in 1807 it caused little anxiety to her merchants.

At the close of the 18th century, however, Bristol was overdependent on the protected sugar and molasses trade with the West Indies. Under the old colonial system Bristol had prospered and her merchants were active within the walls of the old order. Some were still active in the Newfoundland fish trade, and others were beginning to develop commercial links with Canada, but the West India trade alone was worth twice as much to Bristol as all her other overseas commerce combined. It had saved most of the merchant community during the embargoes, shipping losses and bad debts which occurred during the war with the American colonies. It was impossible in 1800 to foresee the total ruin of the sugar islands that was to occur during the next 50 years. The Virginia trade had declined as Glasgow came to dominate the tobacco industry, and commerce with the Caribbean supported Bristol's shipbuilding, provisioning and sugar-refining industries.

Bristol fought and lost many battles in the first half of the 19th century over the defence of the old order. After emancipation in 1833 and Peel's free trade measures, a rapid decline in Bristol's trade with the West Indies occurred. Where there had once been 20 sugar refineries, the last one closed in 1908, but this was part of a larger malaise since the sugar industry continued to thrive in Liverpool and Glasgow. An unenlightened and penny-pinching policy towards Bristol's docks had typified most of the 18th century. It was always the wrong time to do anything about increasing the berthing space, lessening congestion of the port and improving the turn-around time for ships. If trade was depressed it was argued that money invested would not be recoverable; if trade was flourishing, then why invest in dock facilities instead of merchandise? Various schemes to improve the port were put forward from the 1760s which failed to be implemented due to wrong timing, the problems of silting, the need for a tidal bypass, and stagnant city sewage.

The Rev. William Milton, vicar of Temple Church, put forward a plan in 1791 which provided for a dam and lock chamber in the bed of the Avon itself, a new bed for the river along the flat land to Totterdown, and a second cut to take excess flood water and to top up the harbour. His scheme failed because it seemed too costly at a time when the trade of the port was rising again. A very similar scheme to Milton's, however, put forward in December 1802 by Jessop and White, was put into effect between 1804 and 1809, transforming two-and-a-half miles of the old river into a 'floating dock' covering 76 acres of water. A dam and feeder canal at Netham Weir conveyed clean water to the floating harbour and facilitated navigation to Bath.

The City Council then tried to get the money back through increased town dues payable on merchandise coming in to Bristol for sale. In addition, mayor's dues were collected at the quayside by the wardens on all vessels over 60 tons, and wharfage dues, leased to the Society of Merchant Venturers in the 17th century, continued to be collected until 1861. The mayor's dues bore particularly heavily on trade with Ireland and the coasting trade, confining it to smaller, less profitable, vessels. Town dues were 'ad valorem' and caused goods for export to be diverted away from Bristol to Liverpool and the ports of South Wales. In 1848, by Act of Parliament, the Corporation arranged to take over the docks and immediately abolished charges on 530 articles of merchandise. At the end of 10 years of the new management the import trade had increased by 66 per cent, but this very growth in trade, and an increase in the size of boats, forced into greater prominence the natural disadvantages of Bristol as a port.

Sail and wood had begun to give way to steam and iron, and the twists and turns of the six miles up the Avon to the city proved increasingly hazardous. Brunel's *Great Britain* is a case in point, since the stone facings of the locks had to be removed to ease her out into the river. Having built her, Bristolians cheered her down the river but she sailed away to use Liverpool as her port only to return in June 1970. Bristol lost ground as a port for other reasons as well. She never fully recovered her American trade after the American War of Independence. The south-west of England never experienced industrialisation comparable to that of Lancashire which provided such an impetus to Liverpool's growth. Birmingham and the Midlands channelled their exports through Liverpool, rather than Bristol, and in the Severn estuary Bristol suffered the competition of Swansea and later of Cardiff and Newport.

Brunel's great engineering achievements in Bristol are still writ large. The Suspension Bridge, Temple Meads Old Station, the *Great Britain*, and the wrought-iron tubular girder swing bridge spanning his new entrance lock at the docks, all remain as monuments to his genius. Not all of these were recognised as such at the time. Due to lack of supporting capital he never saw the Suspension Bridge completed, and there was much resentment at 'the evil consequences of his pet crochet, the 'broad gauge' system, on the commerce of Bristol ...'. But Bristol did not stand still after Brunel, although the industrial cities of the Midlands and the North had displaced her in population size to 10th place in the table of British cities by 1900. The exploitation of the South Wales coal resources and the growth of the Welsh steel industry and her docks diminished Bristol's importance in the region and some industrial processes disappeared altogether. Coalpit Heath was the last Bristol colliery working in 1939 and was closed in 1949. The Great Western Cotton Works by the Feeder canal at Barton Hill, founded in 1836, which at one time employed more than 1,500 workers, was forced to close in 1925.

Decline affected the famous glass industry which operated 15 glass houses in Bristol in 1800, as well as two more at Nailsea, and it practically ended with the closure of the Phoenix works in Portwall Lane in 1851. Bottle-making continued for another 70 years, concentrated in the Avon Street works of Powell and Ricketts, but was eventually closed in 1923. Soap-making, which had been a leading Bristol industry in the 15th century, survived the vicissitudes of time until the maker of 'Puritan' soap, the Bristol firm of Christopher Thomas Bros. was taken over by William Lever in 1910, and finally closed in 1950. Even such a basic industry to Bristol as shipbuilding, able for so long to produce vessels that were 'shipshape and Bristol fashion' to withstand the rocks in the Avon when the tide was out, could not survive. The lower costs of iron and steel in the northern shipbuilding towns meant that the Bristol yards closed one by one, until, with the closing of the city docks as a port, Charles Hill closed in 1977.

Using census data, Professor Alford's essay on the 19th century draws the conclusion that Bristol 'was a location for many industries and trades but a national centre for almost none'. The other side of the coin, however, is that no firm or industry was large enough for its liquidation to bring about a regional decline. New industries and utilities came to take their place, and mass-production factories in the area began to employ thousands of workers towards the end of the 19th century. In the tobacco industry, chocolate manufacture, the footwear industry, steam engines, waggon and carriage works, motor-cycles, bus and lorry manufacture, chemicals and, above all, aviation, large employers with more heavily-capitalised firms displaced the smaller craft-based industries between the wars.

Bristol Corporation tried radically to restructure the port after taking over the docks in 1848. A new dock was opened at Avonmouth in 1877, and the Portishead dock in 1879. In 1884 all the city's docks were amalgamated into the Port of Bristol Authority, but change had come too late and Midlands industries preferred to send their products elsewhere. Refusing to see itself as a maritime centre in decline, Bristol persisted and opened the Royal Edward Dock in 1908. The deep water port at Avonmouth and the advantage of cheap land attracted the building of the vast Avonmouth zinc complex between 1917 and 1923. The area was also to attract the Imperial Chemicals Industry to a 1,000-acre site after the Second World War. Bristol had been a centre for the chemical industry in the 1830s when Roberts and Daines tar works at Crews Hole, St George, manufactured creosote to preserve the G.W.R. railway sleepers. Later, as William Butler and Co., based at St Philips from 1843-89, it diversified into pitch, benzole, anilene dyes, turpentine, rosin, napthalene, ammonia and, eventually in 1942, lubricating oils, based at Avonmouth. This became part of I.C.I.

Bristol has been, and remains, one of the main locations of the aircraft industry. In 1910, Sir George White founded the Bristol and Colonial Aeroplane Company at Filton. Here the Bristol Boxkite was produced, of which 80 were sold, as was the Bristol fighter plane, which was one of the most successful aircraft in the First World War. The company became Bristol Aeroplane Company, then the British Aircraft Corporation, and then British Aerospace. Over time it has produced the Blenheim bomber, the Beaufighter, the Brabazon, the Concorde, and the Pegasus vectored thrust turbo-fans of the Harrier jump jet.

Concentrated German bombing attacks, beginning on Sunday evening, 24 November 1940, and largely ending on 7 May 1941 caused destruction and damage to the whole area of the city, extending westwards over the castle area to the line formed by High Street and Broad Street. Many medieval churches were destroyed by fire, including St Peter's, St Mary-le-Port, and Temple church. Fire also consumed the finest examples of half-timbered shops and houses remaining in the city, St Peter's hospital and St Mary-le-Port Street. The city began to rebuild when hostilities ended. It continued to diversify its economy and has, since the Second World War, seen an influx of banking, insurance and financial institutions escaping from London's high property rents. These new jobs in the service sector have strengthened Bristol's traditional rôle as the administrative and distribution centre for the western region, alongside its continued commitment to light industry. Perhaps better than most other urban communities Bristol kept alive the spirit of the Merchant Adventurers in its determination to compete and survive.

Bristol has the oldest theatre remaining in this country, founded in 1766. It launched the first provincial newspaper in 1702, and the first provincial partnership bank, known as 'The Old Bank'. In Queen Square, Bristol had the first American Consulate in England. The Public Library, started in 1613 by Robert Redwood, was the first in the provinces, after Norwich. From Bristol John Wesley launched the greatest single religious impetus since the Reformation, and from this same city Mary Carpenter and Hannah More sought to foster a humanitarian commitment which spread far outside the city's boundaries.

Bristol's development throughout the centuries has been directed by a mercantile and civic élite, esoteric and self-perpetuating until the 19th century. As the city docks declined, the location of trading activity shifted to Avonmouth, while the establishment of the new County of Avon in 1974 destroyed Bristol's county status. Destruction of ancient buildings of architectural merit continued after the Second World War: these old photographs of the city remind us that the Blitz of 1941-2 was not the only cause of pointless destruction. The closure of the docks which supplied so much of the maritime character of the city centre is the end of the chapter, but not of the book. Bristol has always retained a diversified structure and continues to succeed because it does so.

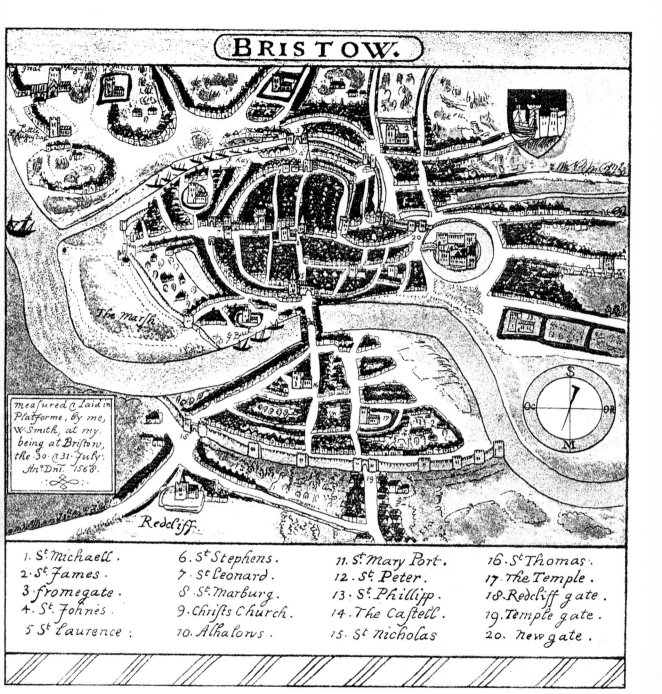

BRISTOW.

*measured & laid in
Platforme, By me,
W. Smith, at my
being at Bristow,
the 30 & 31 July:
An° Dni. 1568.*

1. St Michaell.
2. St James.
3. Fromegate.
4. St Johnes.
5. St Laurence.
6. St Stephens.
7. St Leonard.
8. St Marburg.
9. Chrifts Church.
10. Alhalows.
11. St Mary Port.
12. St Peter.
13. St Phillipp.
14. The Caftell.
15. St Nicholas.
16. St Thomas.
17. The Temple.
18. Redcliff gate.
19. Temple gate.
20. Newgate.

1. William Smith's Plan of Bristol, 1568, is the earliest authentic plan of the city. St Mary Redcliffe is outside the walls. The map shows the new course of the Frome, cut through St Augustine's Marsh 1240-7. William Wyrcester says it formerly flowed from Frome Gate bridge, east of St Stephen's church, along Pill Street and Baldwin Street to join the Avon below Bristol Bridge.

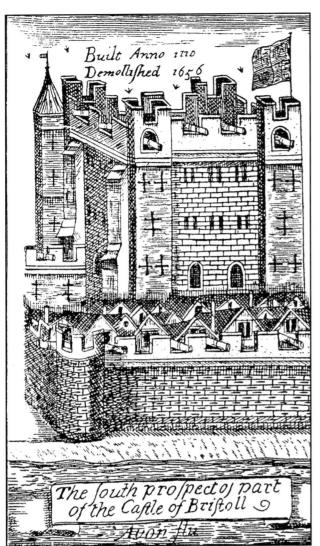

Built Anno 1110
Demolished 1656

The south prospect of part
of the Castle of Bristoll
Avon flu

2. Bristol Castle (built *c*.1110). Millerd's representation of 1673 shows a keep with corner towers, buttresses, and a curtain wall with battlements and towers. The steepled tower of one of the two watchtowers can be seen. Inside the grounds are many roofs of dwelling houses, covering 11 acres. After the Civil War the City Council petitioned Parliament to have it demolished since it had become a refuge for squatters and criminals.

3. A curtain wall tower of Bristol Castle, *c*.1914. This tower was at the rear of 41 Castle Street but was demolished in the 1930s to permit the rebuilding of the street. The outworks of the castle precincts extended to Hlaford's Gate (or Lord's Gate), now Lawford's Gate. The 11 acres covered the area in front of The Galleries and the Holiday Inn.

4. St John's Gate was drawn by Ricart on his map of 1479. A gate and church terminated each of the four main streets of the early medieval city – St John's, New Gate, St Leonard's and St Nicholas'. The old gates had grooves in the sides in which a portcullis was let down. St John's is the only surviving city gate.

5. Robert, third son of Robert Fitzhardinge, gave the church of St Nicholas to the Abbey of St Augustine c.1172. The city gate was beneath the chancel of St Nicholas' church. The removal of the old gateway in 1762 entailed the demolition of most of the church. James Bridges designed an ornate assembly hall with a marvellous ceiling. The old crypt was preserved underneath.

6.   The Haymarket, 1880. This open space was originally connected to St James' churchyard. In 1238 the Bishop of Worcester ordained that a feast of relics should be held yearly at the Priory of St James during the week of Pentecost. By Queen Elizabeth I's reign these fairs were held on 25 July. This is believed to be where plague victims were buried, and is now the site of the John Lewis building.

7. St James' Priory, *c.*1160. The nave has survived as a parish church since 1374. It was originally built by Robert, Earl of Gloucester, on an open site across the river Frome, and made dependent on the earl's great monastery at Tewkesbury. The monks' Choir, the high altar and chapels have gone. The nave that survives was the liturgically less important part of the church, and comprises the five western bays of a six-bay nave.

8. Dominican Friary, *c.*1230. The roof of Bakers' Hall was erected about 1240 and restored in 1974. The building was originally the infirmary of the friary. The Dominicans' buildings were purchased at the Reformation by William Chester, pointmaker, mayor in 1537 and 1552, and M.P. for Bristol in 1555. The timbered roof 49 ft. 3 in. by 24 ft. 3 in., is highly pitched, with curved archbraces beneath the collar beams.

9. The friary eventually passed to Dennis Hollister and became the Quakers Friars meeting house. He was a Quaker, wealthy grocer and M.P. in the Barebones Parliament of 1653. Thomas Callowhill married Hollister's daughter, Hannah. Extreme left is the Cutlers' Hall, originally the dormitory, where cubicles were in line with the lancet windows.

10. Plan of the medieval monastic foundations and churches around the city.

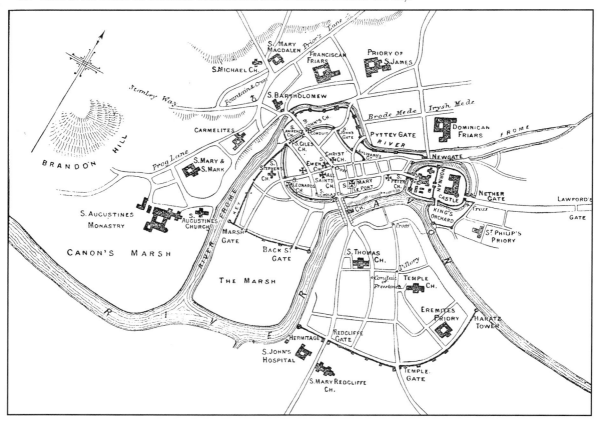

11. The 30 houses and the Chapel of the Assumption on Bristol's medieval bridge survived from 1239 until 1764. The narrow arches restricted the flow of the river and created a weir effect. Bristol's first shops were probably those established in the houses on the bridge, mainly jewellers and mercers by the 14th century.

12. The architect, James Bridges, came from the American colonies in 1756. His plans for Bristol bridge were accepted in 1758 and the trustees appointed him surveyor in 1760. Their lack of confidence, however, caused him to resign and to go to the West Indies. The trustees then went ahead with the design under Thomas Paty's direction, and work was completed in 1768.

13. Due to traffic congestion by 1860 the bridge was widened in autumn 1861 by 12 ft. on the eastern side, by removing the heavy stone battlement and laying a new footpath on iron cantilevers. In 1873-4 the same process was effected on the western side, hiding from view James Bridges' design, but freeing the traffic.

14. Originally Norton's house in Wyrcester's day, St Peter's hospital stood at the top of Castle Green, behind St Peter's. First mentioned in 1402, Robert Aldworth rebuilt two thirds of it and used this as a sugar refinery from 1612. It continued as a sugar house until 1695, became the Bristol Mint and then a hospital for the sick poor. It was destroyed in the Blitz.

15. Jacob Millerd's map, 1673, showing the medieval city. Millerd was a mercer of Bristol and sold his map through Thomas Wall, bookseller. This part of his map shows the ancient walls and gates, the High Cross and St Peter's Cross. The castle site is already covered with houses. Quakers Friars Meeting House is depicted. Around the edge of the map are 20 illustrations of great historical interest.

16. The Pithay, *c*.1850. The well in this street was described by William Wyrcester, and gives the derivation of the name, 'Puit-Hai', or 'Well-close'. The well was drawn by O'Neill for Braikenridge and was 50 ft. deep and 5 ft. across. The Elizabethan half-timbered houses were demolished in 1897 to build J. S. Fry's factory.

17. In old deeds St Mary-le-Port Street was called St Mary de Foro, or St Mary of the Market. This view, *c*.1850, looks towards St Peter's church with Dolphin Street cutting across the middle distance. This narrow street connected the centre of High Street with the centre of Dolphin Street. It was not rebuilt after the Blitz.

18. Barnard's Tobacco, Snuff and Cigar Warehouse, *c.*1900, was in St Mary-le-Port Street. This high pitched double gabled early 17th-century building was demolished on 9 February 1904.

19. William Wyrcester said the Guild of Calendars kept the archives of the town in All Saints' church. Early in the 14th century a disastrous fire in the library destroyed many of the archives. The Tolsey, or covered colonnade, where merchants met to do business, was erected in 1583 and the 'Nails' date from 1594, 1625 and 1631.

20. The view is along Corn Street towards Wine Street. On 27 September 1743 the Exchange was opened. Starting in October 1813 a corn market was held there every Tuesday and Thursday. It was also the appointed place until 1870 for the nomination of Parliamentary candidates and for the declarations of the polls. Corn Street is now pedestrianised.

21. The four brass 'Nails' outside the Exchange were used by merchants in lieu of tables for making payments or writing, hence, 'to pay on the Nail'. Three of the Nails came from the Tolsey alongside All Saints' church. Another Nail came from in front of the Old Council House, and in the 1670s there were six of them.

22.   Built as a residence for a wealthy merchant, this house stood on the corner of High Street and Wine Street from 1676 to 24 November 1940. In 1810 it became the Castle Bank, then, in 1826, Stuckey's Bank. In 1855 it became the property of T. W. Tilley, hatter, who first called it Dutch House. In 1908 it was only saved from demolition by the Lord Mayor's casting vote.

23. John Wesley (1703-91) was a fellow of Lincoln College, Oxford, and missionary to the colony of Georgia from 1735-8. He was 'converted' on 24 May 1738 and came to Bristol in 1739 at the invitation of George Whitefield. Wesley preached his first open-air sermon in England in April 1739. In May he bought land at the Horsefair for the New Room and travelled widely on horseback throughout the country. He ordained his own ministers in 1784 for the American Methodists and thus broke with the Church of England.

24. The New Room in the Horsefair was the first Methodist building in the world. Wesley spent nearly 1,500 nights there from 1739-90. There is a two-decker pulpit. The communion table is that which was used by Wesley. The Common Room upstairs has a plain table and benches, and the doors around lead to study bedrooms for the preachers.

25. Proclamation of George V as king, 14 May 1910. The Lord Mayor, Alderman C. H. Hayes, and the sheriff, George Riseley, are in the ancient proclamation car, at the High Cross, the corner of Corn Street and Broad Street, outside the old Council House. Queen Victoria was proclaimed from seven points of the city, but this was reduced to four in 1910: High Street, the Haymarket, College Green and Queen Square.

26. Wine Street looking east, from Corn Street in the 1920s. Since a pillory once stood at this junction, and a 'winch' (wynch) was on the pillory, 'Wine' could be a corruption of 'wynch'. On the right hand side is the Dutch House and High Street. Behind the Dutch House were Jones' Stores, The Don and Baker Baker. Most of the big stores had premises there. On 24 November 1940 the entire area was destroyed in a raid.

27. During the 1930s many of the older shops were replaced by a series of chain stores. Castle Street was certainly the busiest of Bristol's shopping streets but was blitzed on 24 November 1940. The shopping area was rebuilt in Broadmead.

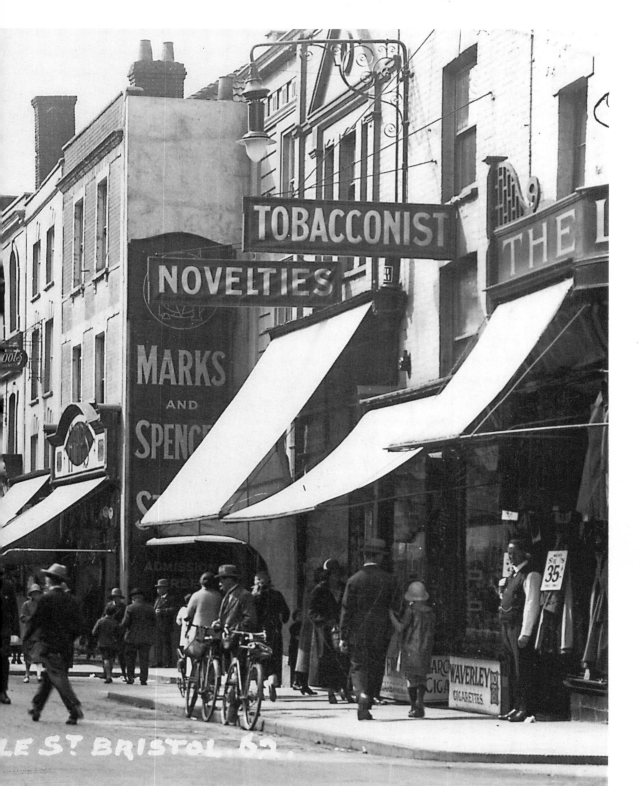

28.   Chocolate factory of J. S. Fry and Sons, Pithay, 1924. The main road junction in the foreground is that between Wine Street and Union Street in the centre of the old town. In 1810, 29 empty old houses in the Pithay were for sale. J. S. Fry had set up a factory in Union Street in 1793. His workforce grew from 11 in 1819 to 350 by 1866. There were 1,000 employees by the 1850s, and 4,600 in 1908. Fry acquired much of the Pithay to extend his factory in 1897.

29.   George's Brewery, 20 September 1920. The site by Bristol Bridge was used for brewing from about 1730. Philip George was manager in 1787 and in 1888 George's became a public company and the largest brewery in the west country. They were absorbed by Courage in 1961.

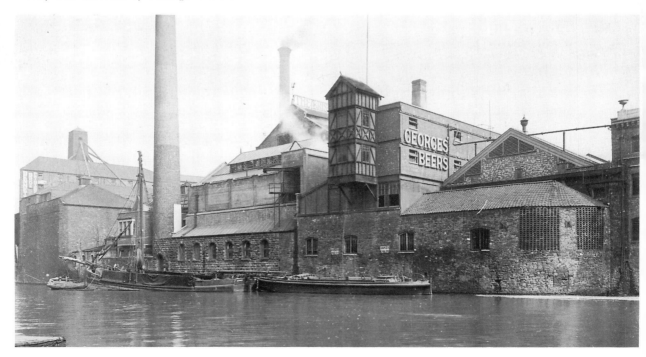

30. Jim Facey's picture, taken from the Odeon Cinema, shows the smoking ruins of Union Street after the raid of 24 November 1940. Seventy fires were reported and some needed five to ten pumping appliances each. Helen Reid has found there were only 224 pumps available, and only enough firemen to man 96 appliances. The rest were manned by part-time firemen.

31. The Dutch House after the raid of 24 November 1940. It appears this bomb fell at 10.20pm. The Dutch House was pulled down by the soldiers two days later. From the photograph it is difficult to see how it could have been restored, although some have said that only the top two floors were damaged.

32. Jones' department store in St Mary-le-Port Street, the morning after the same raid. Jim Facey's picture shows the chef from Jones' working regardless in the ruins. This site is now the Castle car park and was not rebuilt after the war.

33. In the raid of 16 March 1941, 257 people had been killed. In the middle of the air-raid the All Clear was sounded by mistake and people began to leave their shelters. Bombs continued to fall. The Prime Minister visited the city, however, on 12 April to raise morale.

BRISTOW

34. John Speed's plan of Bristol, 1610. Speed was born in Cheshire in 1552. This plan is at the right hand bottom corner of the 1611 map of Gloucestershire.

35. The Harrowing of Hell relief in Bristol Cathedral, c.1050, is the most dramatic evidence of the pre-Conquest church in the city. It is 7 ft. high and was discovered under the chapter house floor; it had been used as a coffin lid. Perhaps the sculpture was meant to be placed over a doorway, since the broadest part is at the feet.

36. William Wyrcester gives the dimensions of the cathedral's Norman chapter house as 71 ft. by 25 ft. There are now only two bays and the room is 42 ft. by 25 ft. as a result of the destruction caused by the 1831 riots. Although truncated, it is still the finest Norman chapter house in the country. The arcaded recesses were used as seats by the monks, but the east wall and window are modern.

37. South choir aisle, c.1330. The choir limb of the cathedral is unique among England's greater churches. The designer managed to convey space because the large windows are in the aisles, which are the same height as the central vault. The outward thrust of the central vault was transmitted to buttresses outside by means of horizontal stone beams, supported by cross arches.

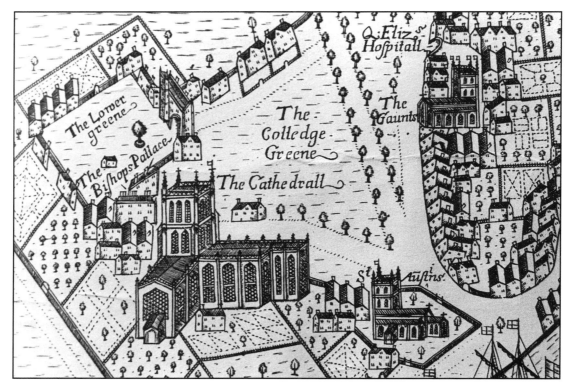

38. The Gaunt's hospital, depicted in Jacob Millerd's map of 1673. At the Dissolution in 1539, and the surrender of the Hospital by John Coleman, most of the buildings went to the king, but the church and the master's residence, Gaunt's House, were bought in 1541 by the corporation. Bristol is the only city in England to have its own corporation chapel.

39. The Lord Mayor's Chapel was used from 1590 by Queen Elizabeth's Hospital School, which had been founded by John Carr, whitesoap maker. In 1769 Queen Elizabeth's hospital was removed by Alderman Dampier and the city corporation to the St Bartholomew's hospital. Bristol Grammar School, founded 1531 by Nicholas Thorne, moved from St Bartholomew's to Gaunt's hospital, until its move to Tyndall's Park in 1879. The headmaster of Bristol Grammar School, the Rev. Charles Lee, was the son-in-law of Alderman Dampier, and remained headmaster for 47 years.

40. St Stephen's parish was created as a result of the enlargement of the town in 1239-40, when a new bed for the Frome was cut through St Augustine's Marsh. The Shipward family rebuilt nearly all of St Stephen's church in the Perpendicular style, with a clerestory. Inside are the tombs of Martin Pring and Edward Blanket.

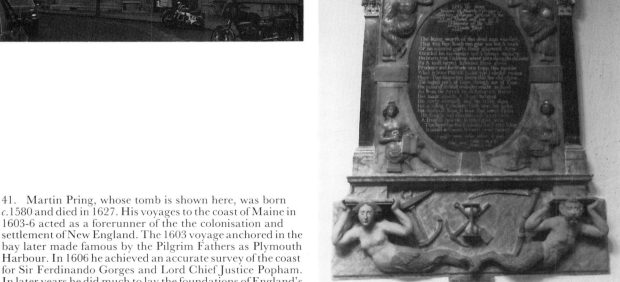

41. Martin Pring, whose tomb is shown here, was born c.1580 and died in 1627. His voyages to the coast of Maine in 1603-6 acted as a forerunner of the the colonisation and settlement of New England. The 1603 voyage anchored in the bay later made famous by the Pilgrim Fathers as Plymouth Harbour. In 1606 he achieved an accurate survey of the coast for Sir Ferdinando Gorges and Lord Chief Justice Popham. In later years he did much to lay the foundations of England's connections with India.

42. The Great House, St Augustine's Back, c.1860. Sir John Young started building the house in 1568, and it was completed in time to house Queen Elizabeth I for a week in 1574. Forty rooms were laid out round a rectangle. Sugar was made here until 1797, when Edward Colston bought the house. He turned it into a school – Colston Boys' School – which occupied the house until 1861.

43. Originally called Knifesmiths Street, Christmas Street had been a precipitous footpath until 1669. Alderman Jonathan Blackwell, a wealthy vintner, built proper steps at his own expense, called Queen Street. At the foot of Christmas Steps, on the right, is the entrance to St Bartholomew's hospital, founded by sailors at some time before 1207.

44. Steep Street in the 1850s. Sited just above the city centre these unhygienic and cluttered buildings were a prime target for slum clearance, and were removed by the Streets Improvement Committee in 1871. A fierce hand-to-hand struggle took place in this area after the surrender of the city by Colonel Fiennes to Prince Rupert.

45. Host Street was to be found off Colston Street and ran behind Colston Avenue. Pictured here in the 1850s it comprised 17th-century buildings and a cobbled street. Hugh Owen, who photographed this view and also no.44, conveys the alley-like claustrophobic character of these overhanging storeys.

46. There had been a High Cross on the High Street/Corn Street site in 1247, but a new and splendid one was erected in 1373 to commemorate Bristol's county status. In 1633 another tier was added, raising it to 39 ft. 6 in. Removed to College Green in 1733, it was sold to Henry Hoare of Stourhead in 1763.

47. Philip Vandyke was a painter who came to Bristol from the Netherlands and settled here. He is best known for his likenesses of Coleridge and Southey. He painted Clare Street, which had been built 1771-5, the drawbridge and the quay *c*.1780. On the further side of the drawbridge is a night watchman's hut.

48. St Augustine's Parade, looking towards the drawbridge, *c.*1865, showing horse-drawn cabs at the entrance to what is now Canon's Road. These were replaced by motor taxis, which charged 8d. a mile in 1908. An Irish boat lies alongside the Dublin Shed. The small tower once carried signals to shipping when it was clear to leave the harbour.

49. St Augustine's, the swing bridge and Stone Bridge, *c.*1880. In 1892 the river Frome beyond the swing bridge was covered over, and the water in the foreground covered in 1938. Three churches are visible, St Mary's on the Quay with the classical portico, the spire of St John on the Wall, and the City church, St Stephen's, to the right.

50.   The open River Frome and Stone Bridge, 1885. The picture shows a glimpse through to Georgian Rupert Street. In the centre is the figurehead from the SS *Demarara* which broke her back in the River Avon in 1851, while on her maiden voyage. In 1893 this scene was lost when the River Frome was culverted. The statues of Burke and Colston were erected soon afterwards.

51.   Culverting of the Frome began on 11 May 1892 from the Stone Bridge, Rupert Street to the junction of Clare Street and Baldwin Street, and was finished on 6 May 1893. In the space created by culverting, the mayor, Sir Charles Wathen, organised an Industrial Exhibition in a wooden building 520 ft. long by 110 ft. wide. This was opened by the then mayor, R. H. Symes, on 23 August 1893 and closed on 31 January 1894.

52. This picture of the tramway centre was taken after the Frome had been culverted as far as Clare Street, probably *c.*1899, as the tramway centre was constructed over the area. Horse-drawn traffic still prevails.

53. The tramway centre after 1908. The C.W.S. building has been built on the left. An Irish boat is drawn alongside the Dublin Shed. The triangular area in the centre of the picture was known as 'Skivvys' Island' because of the large number of cleaning ladies who waited here for their trams back home.

54. Trams could usually be drawn by two horses on level roads, but Bristol is a hilly city and on the steeper hills extra power was supplied by trace horses, shown here in Park Street *c.*1885. These were kept in readiness at strategic points. There was no covering for outside passengers and, before 1894, women could not use the vertical, spiral iron steps to the top deck with any decorum.

55. Junction between Clare Street and Baldwin Street, *c*.1890. The trams are still horse-drawn, and Thornley's hat shop on the corner has not yet been demolished to build the new Sun, Fire and Life Insurance Offices (the architect of which was Sir George Oatley). Clare Street was the main thoroughfare to the city centre via Bristol Bridge before Baldwin Street was opened in 1881.

56. St Augustine's Parade and Colston Street, 1913. The Hippodrome was built on the site of Smith and Co. Home Furnishers, at 13 St Augustine's Parade, and opened 16 December 1912. The Bristol Gas Building, next to the Colston Hall, was built in 1906.

57. In the late 18th century there were 35 importers of wines and vintners in Bristol. Harveys, Averys and J. R. Phillips are the best known. William Perry set up a wine merchant's business in Denmark Street in 1794. Thomas Harvey, a ship's captain, carried Perry's wine. Perry and Urch took Thomas Harvey's son, John, into business when he was aged 14, and the firm became John Harvey and Sons in 1871. Harvey's cellars in Denmark Street are seen here in the 1930s.

58.   15 July 1939 was the very last chance to see trams in the city centre. Three trams were waiting at five minutes past midday outside the Tramway Offices, and a motorbus has just left the stop. There are few cars, but at least six bicycles.

59. Broad Quay, Bristol, *c*.1735. This painting shows the massive new channel for the River Frome, dug across St Augustine's Marsh 1240-7. The trench was some 2,400ft. long, 120ft. wide, and 18ft. deep. The quay was cobbled and hogsheads of rum and molasses were pulled on sledges because of all the cellars beneath. Hand cranes were used.

60. William Canynge's house, 93 Redcliffe Street dated from the 14th century, but was destroyed in 1937 when the road was widened. It had a fine arch-braced hall roof. A superb fireplace, richly carved, depicts Canynge as a merchant, and as dean of Westbury College; this has been preserved in the Bristol Savages' Wigwam. Canynge feasted Edward IV in the banqueting hall of this great house.

61. The Merchants' Hall was formerly the disused Chapel of St Clement, which was granted to the Society of Merchants by the Corporation in 1493. It stood on the corner of King Street, near Broad Quay. In Millerd's map of 1673 it is shown as a plain and unpretentious building. The hall was reconstructed in 1693 and from 1719-22 nearby property was purchased.

62. In 1787 major alterations taking several years were made to the Merchants' Hall: the architect was Thomas Paty. The old front was replaced by a pretentious, decorated façade. It was destroyed in the raid of 6 December 1940, and hit again on 8 May 1941 when a hundred high explosive bombs were dropped and 78 fires started.

63. St Mary Redcliffe church lost its spire in a gale of 1445. This was not replaced until restoration began in 1858 when this photograph was taken. In 1872, the new spire was completed, and the mayor, Alderman Proctor Baker, climbed to the top and laid the capstone.

64. St Mary Redcliffe is the finest example of Gothic architecture in England. On 13 July 1588, Queen Elizabeth I gave back lands confiscated by Edward VI, to pay for its upkeep. Built on the red cliff outside the city walls, there was a church on the site in 1180, and parts of it are incorporated. The building of the present church began in 1280, and by 1380 it was largely complete.

65. The memorial tablet to Sir William Penn (1621-70) in St Mary Redcliffe consists of three streamers flown from his ships, his Admiral's crest, helmet, breast plate, gauntlets, dagger and spurs. The Red Flag of one of Cromwell's Generals also hangs there. Penn was Commander-in-Chief of the fleet against Spain and also against the Dutch. He captured Jamaica and was knighted by Charles II in 1660.

66. On Whitsunday, the mayor and Corporation attend St Mary Redcliffe in full civic costume and the church is strewn with rushes and flowers. This custom dates from 1494 when William Mede, three times mayor, gave a tenement on the Back to the Corporation, the rent of which was to pay for an annual sermon on the feast of Pentecost.

I who was Born a PAGAN and a SLAVE
Now Sweetly Sleep a CHRISTIAN in my Grave
What tho my hue was dark my SAVIOR'S sight
Shall Change this darkness into radiant light
Such grace to me my Lord on earth has given
To recommend me to my Lord in heaven
Whose glorious second coming here I wait
With saints and Angels Him to celebrate

67. The gravestone of Scipio Africanus is to be found in Henbury churchyard. Scipio was a negro boy of 18 who died on 21 December 1720. On the head and foot are the heads of black cherubs. He was servant to the Earl of Suffolk and Arabella (née Astry), who both died within four months of Scipio. Several other negroes are buried in Bristol graveyards; some, for example, in the Strangers' Burial Ground, Clifton.

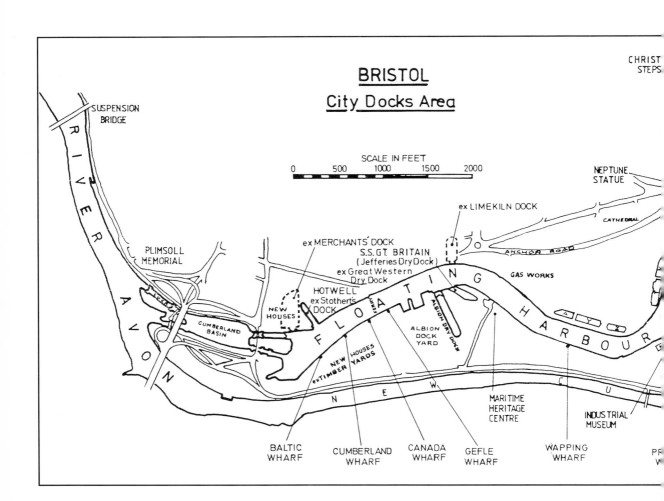

BRISTOL
City Docks Area

68. The *Jason* privateer. A pen-and-ink drawing by Nicholas Pocock, *c*.1760. The details of the loading and taking of slaves suggest Pocock had direct experience of the slave trade. The *Jason* was built in 1747 at Bayonne, in France, and was probably captured soon afterwards, since in 1748 she was sailing as a Bristol privateer. She carried 32 guns, 200 men and displaced 350 tons.

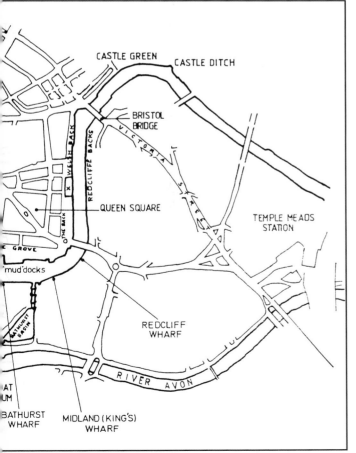

69. Map of Bristol city docks.

70. John Padmore's great crane, *c*.1735. Padmore, of Bath, built his crane on the Old or West Mud Dock, known as Great Dock, where there were four berths, near the end of Prince Street. The three jibs of the crane were worked by treadmills, housed in the long shed and raised on 14 cast-iron clad pillars. Morticed cogs around the outside rim of the treadmills permitted effective braking.

71. The *Southwell* frigate, also drawn by Pocock. By October 1746 the *Southwell* was used as a slave ship, but held Letters of Marque enabling her to take part in privateering. She was one of the largest of Bristol's ships, displacing 400 tons, with 24 guns, 200 men and 14 swivel guns. In 1746, the *Southwell* arrived in Antigua with 301 slaves, having lost 150 on the crossing.

72a. & b. In 1802 Jessop submitted plans to convert the old bed of the River Avon into 73 acres of non-tidal harbour. His original and final plans are shown here. Cumberland Basin was dug through Rownham Meads in 1804-9.

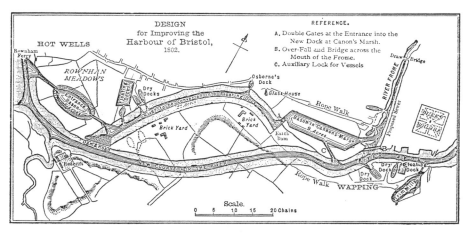

DESIGN
for Improving the
Harbour of Bristol,
1802.

REFERENCE.

A. Double Gates at the Entrance into the New Dock at Canon's Marsh.
B. Over-Fall and Bridge across the Mouth of the Frome.
C. Auxiliary Lock for Vessels

Scale.
0   5   10   15   20 Chains

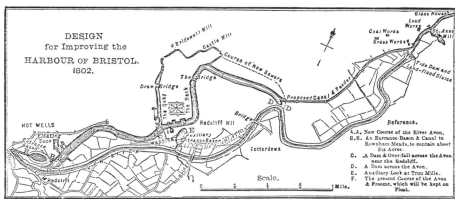

DESIGN
for Improving the
HARBOUR OF BRISTOL.
1802.

Reference.
A.A. New Course of the River Avon.
B.B. An Entrance-Bason & Canal to Rownham-Meads, to contain about Six Acres.
C. A Dam & Over-fall across the Avon, near the Redcliff.
D. A Dam across the Avon.
E. Auxiliary-Lock at Trim Mills.
F. The present Course of the Avon & Froome, which will be kept on Float.

Scale.
0   ¼   ½   ¾   1 Mile.

73. This photograph shows Cumberland Basin, c.1965. The New Cut is that nearest to the camera. In the foreground are three large tobacco bonds, built in 1906, 1908 and 1919. A new road complex was opened here in 1965: a flyover crosses the basin.

74.   Rownham ferry and the entrance to Cumberland Basin, *c*.1862. Jessop's north entrance lock is to the left and Brunel's lock (built 1844-9 to replace Jessop's south entrance lock) is on the right. Brunel's lock, 262 ft. long and 52 ft. wide, is now sealed by a concrete wall. At low tide, when there was not enough water to row, several gang planks were laid across small boats. It was closed in 1933.

75.   Bristol city docks, in 1965. Cumberland Basin is in the foreground and the New Cut is on the right. The Merchants' Dock is in the middle of the picture, and opposite is the Underfall Yard. On the bend at the top, on the right, are Hill's shipyard and Great Western Dock.

76. Shipping at The Grove, *c.*1870, viewed from Redcliffe Parade, and looking towards Prince Street Bridge which was then a double leaf swing bridge. On the left is the partially dismantled Guineaman *Look Out*. Opposite are the East and West Mud Docks and Guinea St Ferry slip. The Nova Scotia barque *Emma Parker* is alongside The Grove.

77.   The Fairbairn Steam Crane was ordered from Stothert and Pitt, of Bath, in 1875, and was capable of lifting 35 tons. The curved jib of the crane was 40 ft. high and 15 ft. long. As the size of the ships increased it could not reach over sufficiently far to lift boilers or engines for repair and was superseded.

78.   The Grove, *c*.1880. Bathurst Wharf and Shed (1867 and 1875) are on the left, and were originally Upper Railway Wharf. On the right, Hide Shed (1863-4), later named Severn Shed, is the oldest surviving shed in the city docks. The Bush Tea Warehouse is in the centre background.

79. The docks, *c.*1912, were still busy although the increasing size of vessels had necessitated improved berthing facilities at Avonmouth. On the right are the timber yards of Baltic, Gefle and Canada Wharves. This is now a housing development. On the left is Hotwells Road where the new Rownham Mead housing development occupies the waterfront.

80. Welsh Back and Redcliffe Back, 25 April 1924. Many of the buildings on the right bank were destroyed in the Blitz. The dockside warehouses of Redcliffe Back remain. The one with the pediment is the 1913 Western Counties Agriculture Co-op, and the next two are Buchanan's Warehouses (1883-4). Bottom, left bank, is Hide Shed.

81. The floating harbour in the 1930s seen from the corporation granary. On the left is Railway Wharf with the Fairbairn steam crane, and 'Z' Shed on the right is equipped with electric roof cranes. The *Boston City* is tethered alongside 'Z' Shed. It was built for the Bristol City Line in 1920 at the Albion Dockyard.

82. Old Granary, Welsh Back, 1871. This fine 10-storey building in hard Cattybrook bricks was designed by A. Ponton and W. V. Gough for Messrs. Wait and James. Since it was a granary the patterned brickwork openings were necessary for ventilation. At the corners inside were the lifts for delivering the sacks to the various floors, and also to the waiting carts below, through the round holes under the first floor string course.

83. Redcliffe Hill Shot Tower was one of the earliest brick-built houses in Bristol and the first shot tower in the world. It was demolished in 1969 for road widening. In December 1782, William Watts, a plumber, was granted a patent for his new process. He began to extend his house upwards by two storeys and dug through the cellars and a well below to achieve the necessary drop of 120ft. He made a fortune of £10,000 but became bankrupt in 1794.

84. Charles Hill and Company's yards, seen from Hotwells, c.1968. The railway line from the dockside to Canon's Marsh has now been removed. The marina and Albion Yard began life as the New Dockyard, owned by Hilhouse and Sons. In 1848 the company became Charles Hill and the dock was renamed Albion. Charles Hill and Company closed in 1977, because of the closure of the city docks.

85. SS *War Quince*, pictured on 17 April 1919, displaced 2,499 tons, and was one of eight such standard merchant ships of that tonnage built at the yard in the years 1918-19 for the British Government. In fact 24 ships of over 1,000 tons were constructed at Albion Dockyard between 1915 and 1925.

86. St Nicholas' Almshouses were the first buildings to be erected in King Street, in 1652. Land added in 1656 included a round bastion and part of the outer city wall. When excavating to build a new wing for flats in the late 1950s the old town wall was revealed, and it is preserved in the courtyard. The almshouses were restored in 1961.

87. Merchant Venturers' Almshouses, King Street. The Gild of Mariners had existed in the 16th century and met in the Chapel of St Clement. When Edward VI suppressed chantries the Gild was dissolved, but the Gild's property was granted in 1553 to the first Master of the Merchant Venturers, Edward Prin. A penny in the pound was deducted from sailors' wages to maintain an almshouse and free school for mariners' children, next to St Clement's. A new building was added in 1696.

88. The Theatre Royal in King Street opened on 30 May 1766. The architect was James Paty. In 1800 the ceiling was raised to permit a gallery, but some of the original seating has been retained until today. The 1903 entrance was designed by Pope and Skinner and the houses on the left had to be demolished. To the right of the theatre is Coopers' Hall, built 1743, and now the foyer.

89. Llandoger Trow stands on the corner of King Street and Queen Charlotte Street. This row originally contained five gabled houses, only the last of which was an inn. A 'Trow' was a sailing barge which travelled between Welsh Back and Llandoger in the Wye Valley. The inn is linked with Daniel Defoe and Alexander Selkirk, and was patronised by Henry Irving.

90. In 1774 Elias Vanderhorst, from South Carolina, settled in Bristol with his family and established himself as a merchant. President George Washington appointed him Britain's first consul for the new U.S.A. in 1792 and the consulate was at 37 Queen Square, shown here. The document appointing him, signed by George Washington and Thomas Jefferson, can be seen in the Record Office.

91. Queen Square, St Augustine's Reach, The Grove, The Backs. Queen Square was built between 1699 and 1727. In the 1831 riots all the houses of the north row and most of those on the west were burnt down. At the bottom centre is the Bush Tea Warehouse, built in two sections, c.1832 and 1837, and now the Arnolfini Gallery. Queen Square was bisected by Redcliffe Way in the 1930s.

THE TOBACCO AND SNUFF MANUFACTORY OF MESSRS. W. D. AND H. O. WILLS AND SONS, REDCLIFF STREET, BRISTOL.

92.   W. D. and H. O. Wills and Sons, Redcliffe Street. The first H. O. Wills came to Bristol in 1786 and joined Samuel Watkins as a partner in a tobacco manufacturing business at 73 Castle Street with eight employees. There were then 14 other tobacco firms in the area. The firm moved to this factory at 112 Redcliffe Street in 1791. H. O. Wills died in 1826, and his two sons, W. D. and H. O., took over the business. Both were non-smokers.

93.   Tobacco bonds, warehousing unmanufactured tobacco before paying duty. The Port of Bristol Authority has three tobacco warehouses at Cumberland Basin. The bonds at Canon's Marsh were constructed between 1931 and 1935 and demolished on 29 May 1988 (No.9 bond). The warehousing in Winterstoke Road, built in 1937, has accommodation for 50,000 hogsheads and constitutes No.4 bond. Before 1939 Burgess Tobacco Warehouses, Nos.10 and 11 bonds, were in Anchor Road, and Chard's No.5 bond was in Gasferry Lane.

94. Wadham, Ricketts and Co., glassmakers of Bristol, 1790. In 1722 there were 15 glasshouses in Bristol, in 1794, 12, and by 1830 the number had fallen to four. The Phoenix glasshouse in Portwall Lane, outside Temple Gate, was the last to be built in Bristol. There were in 1789 three flint glasshouses in Bristol; the one at Bedminster was closing down and probably provided the skilled labour. The Phoenix took over its other competitor on Redcliffe Backs in 1802, but closed in 1851.

95. Isaac Jacobs was a glassmaker c.1806-21, eventually being declared bankrupt because of the Napoleonic War and the American War of 1812-14. In 1787 the business started by his father, Lazarus, was in Avon Street, St Philip's. The billhead shows the cones and sailing ships, representing his substantial trade in flint glass. The business sent a dessert set to the King in 1806.

96. H. and T. Proctor's glass cone, *c*.1925. Glasshouses were very conspicuous, being about 90 ft. high and 50 ft. diameter inside. Taken from St Mary Redcliffe, this picture shows how close the church was to shunting yards and trucks. The Prewitt Street glass cone behind St Mary's was taken over in 1812 by H. and T. Proctor for the manufacture of chemicals and artificial fertilisers.

97. Another view of the Prewitt Street cone, which was said to have been the largest built. It now houses a restaurant.

98. SS *Great Britain*, designed by Isambard Kingdom Brunel, was launched in 1843. She was built of wrought iron and fitted with a screw propellor. After four return crossings of the Atlantic she ran aground off Ireland and was salvaged a year later. For 23 years she took passengers to Australia. In 1882 she was converted to a sailing ship, and eventually became a store for coal and wool in the Falklands. In 1970 she was towed back to Bristol.

99. SS *Great Britain* was towed the 7,500 miles back to Bristol from Port Stanley, in the Falkland Islands, by the tug *Varius II* (724 tons) on the salvage pontoon *Mulus III* (2,667 tons). They arrived off Avonmouth on 22 June 1970 and here they are entering, on 25 June, Royal Edward Dry Dock. The gravity dock was used to sink the pontoon and refloat the ship. A massive steel plate had to be welded behind the crack on the starboard side before Lloyds would grant a towing certificate.

100. On 19 July the *Great Britain* was inched gently back into her original dock.

101. This photograph of Isambard Kingdom Brunel possibly was taken by Robert Howlett (1831-88). He stands with Earl Derby who in 1858 was president of the Board of Trade and Secretary of State for India, and with John Scott Russell, F.R.S., in whose Napier Yard, Isle of Dogs, the Great Eastern was built. He is watching the Great Eastern slide down the slipway.

102. Jacob Millerd's map showing the parish of Temple, which was south of the river. The map shows Temple church, the racks for drying, Tucker Street, Bristol Bridge with its Chapel of the Assumption and houses, the Temple Cross near the Counterslip, and, just outside the walls, St Mary Redcliffe.

103. Relics of Templar's oval church of 1154 are under Temple church, Victoria Street. Temple church did not become Holy Cross parish church until 1339 after the Templars had been suppressed in the 14th century. In 1307 the king sold their property to the Knights of St John of Jerusalem. The Knights built the present church on alluvial soil, and the tower leaned 3 ft. 9 in. from the perpendicular.

104. Temple gate stood at the top of Temple Street and impeded traffic. It was rebuilt in 1734 with an extremely narrow roadway for carriages, and two passageways for pedestrians. Rather than accommodate the gate to the traffic, the corporation regulated the traffic to the gate. Entry of wains and carts with iron-bound wheels was banned on pain of a 6s.8d. fine. In 1808 the gate was in a ruinous state and was dismantled.

105. William Fifield's painting for J. D. Pountney shows Temple Back Pottery on 15 February 1820, looking towards Temple church from the south. Two biscuit kilns, the throwing room, two glazing kilns, the printing shop, and the chimney of the hardening kiln are visible. Pountney's moved to St Philip's Marsh in 1884, and then to Fishponds in 1905 until 1969.

106. Brunel's G.W.R. office buildings, built in 1839-41. The neo-Tudor style façade in Bath stone originally housed, on the first floor, the board room, and the residence of the station superintendent. On the ground floor was the public booking office for the Paddington to Bristol line, which opened in June 1841. The building has been little altered, but was cleaned in 1990.

107. Brunel's train shed (c.1840s) at Temple Meads has been preserved by B.R, substantially as seen in this lithograph by John Bourne. It is the most important terminus station from the early railway era and is built on vaulting 15 ft. above the ground level. The train shed has a 72 ft. centre span, cantilevered wooden roof, over four tracks.

108. Temple Meads in the 1860s. The Bristol and Exeter offices are in the centre distance, and the wooden structure on the left, known as the 'cow shed', was the terminus of the B. & E.R. line. Brunel's G.W.R. train shed is on the right. The tracks in the foreground show the Brunel 7 ft. gauge and the 4 ft. 8½ in. standard gauge. Broad gauge G.W.R. rolling stock is on the right hand side.

109. Sir Mathew Digby Wyatt was architectural adviser to all three railway companies which co-operated to build a joint station on the site of the old Bristol and Exeter station in 1865. The original Brunel building was extended eastwards and a connecting curve joined the almost separate new station to the old. S. C. Fripp's neo-Jacobean B. & E.R. offices of 1852 remain.

110. Lavar's panoramic view of Bristol from the south, 1887. Nadar had produced a similar view in 1858 by taking a photograph from a balloon. Queen Square, with St Augustine's Reach and the drawbridge, is to the left. Old Market, St Philip's and Temple Meads are to the right. Totterdown Lock and the entrance to the Feeder Canal are bottom right.

111. Temple Meads. In the central triangle can be seen the neo-Jacobean B.&E.R. offices and, immediately above, the offices and platform extensions of Old Station, dating from 1840 and 1878. By the 1920s more than 500 trains a day were using the station, and by 1935 five new platforms had been added on the down side. Above the station are the covered goods depots.

112. Christopher Thomas and Sons' soap works, Broad Plain, c.1845.

113. Christopher Thomas and Sons' soap works. In 1841 the firm of Samuel Fripp and Joseph Fry merged with Thomas Thomas. The present Gardiner's building off Broad Plain housed (from c.1845) the newly-merged factory under the name Christopher Thomas. In the early Stuart period there were 183 soap boilers in Bristol, but the policy of monopolies under Charles I reduced the number to four. In the 1870s Christopher Thomas produced eight per cent of the national total, making 13,000 tons of soap a year. The firm was taken over in 1910 by William Lever, and production finally ceased in 1950.

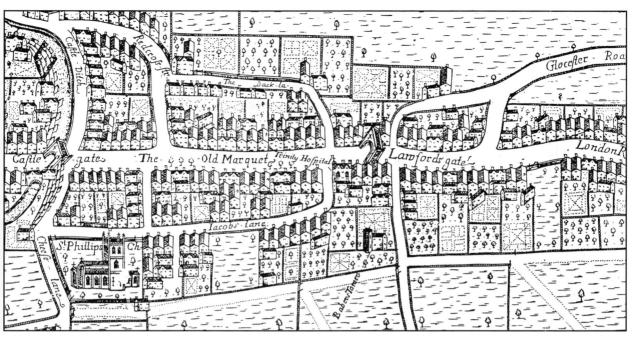

114. The Old Market area, shown here on Jacob Millerd's map of 1673, is outside the 11-acre castle site. The constable's officials collected tolls from traders at Lawford's Gate, and it was already known as Old Market in the 12th century. The broad thoroughfare was used for the market, so travellers had to revert to the Back Lane and Jacob's Lane.

115. The Pieds Poudreux ('Pie Powder') court was established at the *Stag and Hounds*, Old Market, from 1483. Here the Law Merchant was administered on a daily basis for traders at the Old Market Fair. The court of the 'dusty feet' came into existence in the 13th century and originally had met in the open air. The court was discontinued after 1870 when the Crown court took over from the old Tolsey.

116. Old Market, *c.*1913. The *Stag and Hounds*, halfway up the road on the right, forms the boundary of Old Market alongside an underpass. Almost opposite, Carey's Lane opens into Old Market beyond the Empire, on the left, and from there forwards everything has been removed and replaced. Electric trams first left Old Market on 14 October 1895.

117. Built beside St Philip Bridge in 1904 in classical style, the tramway generating station provided power for a fleet of 237 trams running on 31 route miles of track. The service finally closed on 11 April 1941, when a bomb destroyed St Philip's Bridge which carried the power cables. Today the generating station still stands as part of Courage's brewery.

118. Central Electricity lighting station, St Philip's Bridge. Built in 1891-3, this was originally the engine house. There were two large chimneys, each 180 ft. high and 9 ft. across, but they have since been demolished. It housed 18 coal-fired steam engines. In 1882 Bristol Council obtained powers to prevent private companies from providing electricity. The station was municipally owned from the outset.

119. Like most of the city churches, Temple church was locked and unprotected on the night of Sunday, 24 November 1940. As the incendiary bombs fell, firefighters could not enter and the church's fate was sealed once it was well alight. During the night 207 were killed, 187 seriously wounded, 703 slightly injured, and 1,390 rendered homeless in Bristol. This picture shows Victoria Street and Temple church on the morning after the raid.

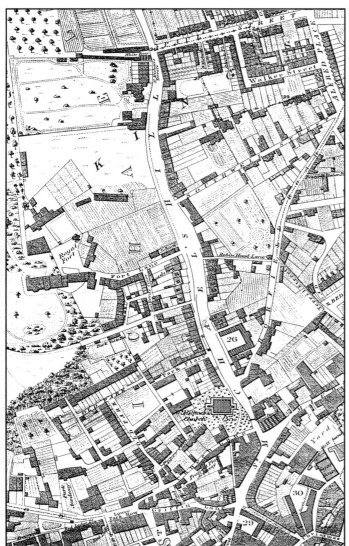

120. St Michael's Hill, shown here on Ashmead's map of 1828, is an example of ribbon development. The more wealthy merchants moved from the medieval city in the 17th century, up St Michael's Hill, Upper Clifton, or Kingsdown. This street has an interesting variety of styles from 16th-century timber-framed houses to Victorian town houses. Short frontages, raised pavements and railings are features.

121. Millerd's map of 1673 shows some 16th-century houses on St Michael's Hill which are still there. They have gables and stepped storeys.

122. Edward Colston erected these almshouses on St Michael's Hill in 1691 for 12 men and 12 women who were not 'drunkards' nor those 'of a vicious life', but who lived in 'some sort of decency'. Each person in the house was to receive 24 sacks of coal and 10 shillings for soap and candles each year. Colston's almshouses are now in the care of the Merchant Venturers.

123. A splendidly preserved town house on St Michael's Hill (dating from 1711) with a fanlight, pediment, platband, and an attic storey, represents the substantial construction taking place at this time. The town was now spreading out to Cotham and Upper Kingsdown and similar houses were being built there.

124. The Old Pump Room, Hotwells. The hot springs emerged on both sides of the Avon. Milky white water gushed out at 76°F. In April 1695 the Merchant Venturers leased the well for 90 years to Thomas Callowhill, draper, and Charles Jones, soapboiler, who were required to build a pump room and lodging houses for visitors. The building looked more like a dock warehouse than a spa.

125. In 1820 the Merchant Venturers decided to try to increase their income from the Hotwell by erecting a new pump room, four veined marble baths and a marble fountain. This was opened in 1822. They disposed of it to the Corporation when it was decided to improve navigation on the Avon by removing Hotwell Point. The buildings were demolished in 1867.

126. One of the most spectacular terraces in Clifton, begun in 1791 by James Lockier across the former gardens and orchard of the Rev. John Power's mansion, was Royal York Crescent. At the west end the terrace is 20 ft. above the road. Lockier was declared bankrupt in March 1793, and the Crescent was not completed until 1820. There are 46 brick-built houses with a total of 146 bays.

127. Map of Clifton and Hotwells.

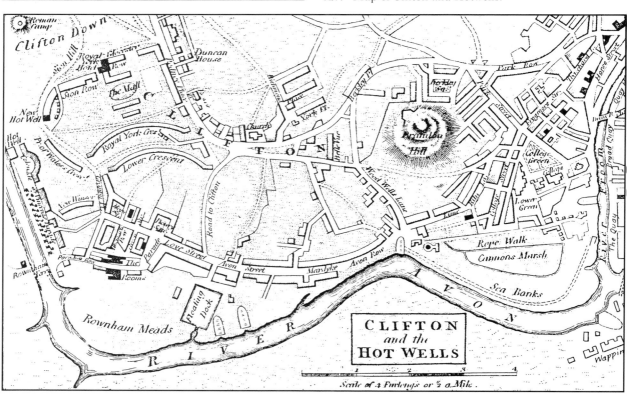

128. Windsor Terrace, Clifton.
Rownham Woods was leased in 1790 by
William Watts, plumber, who spent the
fortune he had derived from the patent for
making shot, on a retaining wall and
vaulting necessary to level the site. Watts
was declared bankrupt in March 1794. By
1809 John Drew had completed 10 houses
to a much reduced design.

129. The amazing variety of rocks,
fossils, ores and stones which make up the
grotto to Goldney House, took Thomas
Goldney 20 years to assemble. It is among
the most elaborate examples surviving,
and was built from 1737 to 1764. His
father had been the principal partner in
Captain Woodes-Rogers' voyage round
the world (1708-11), which brought back
a great quantity of treasure.

130. No. 6 Dowry Square, c.1725, is an oddity, with a tiny frontage squeezed into the corner with two façades. Here Dr. Thomas Beddoes, Reader in Chemistry at Oxford (1788-92), set up his 'Pneumatic Institution' to treat diseases by inhalation. Beddoes' assistant was Humphrey Davy, the inventor of the miners' lamp, who also experimented with nitrous oxide as a means of anaesthesia. His apparatus was constructed by James Watt and partly paid for by Thomas Wedgwood.

131. Lower Clifton became an industrialised area in the 17th century with shipping trades, a brickyard, a glasshouse, the Limekiln Dock and numerous limeburners. The Hotwell Road was widened in 1849, and is pictured here c.1900, looking west. From Dowry Square to Anchor Road there were, by 1901, 53 different trades: 23 pubs, 10 butchers, three fishmongers, 12 greengrocers, 10 bakers, five tailors, six tobacconists, three drapers, two hairdressers, six grocers and two chemists.

132. In 1753 William Vick left £1,000 to accrue interest, to build a bridge across the Gorge. By 1830 the sum had reached £8,000, but Brunel's scheme eventually cost £57,000. In 1831 Lady Elton turned the first sod, and the Marquess of Northampton laid the foundation stone on the Somerset side in 1836.

133. Clifton Suspension Bridge. Work was abandoned in 1843 when £40,000 had been spent. Brunel died four years before work to link the towers commenced, in 1859. A new company was formed in 1861 which acquired the towers and approaches for £2,000. Chains were purchased from the Hungerford Bridge, London, which Brunel had completed in 1843; a third chain was added to each side, and anchored 70ft. into solid rock. Clifton Suspension Bridge finally opened in 1864.

134.   Sir George Oatley's sketches show that the Wills Memorial Building was designed in 1911. The University had received its Charter in 1909 and in 1912 Sir G. A. Wills and H. H. Wills offered to finance a new building. The tower is over 200 ft. high and 55 ft. square, while the entrance hall is 72 ft. high. It was completed in 1925.

135.   The Gothic Wills University tower dominates the surrounding area. Berkeley Square, designed by Thomas and William Paty (1787-90), is on the left. Beyond the University tower is Bristol Grammar School, on Tyndall's Park since 1879.

136.   Started in 1897 on the fourth centenary of Cabot's sighting of North America, Cabot Tower on Brandon Hill was designed by W. V. Gough. John Cabot and his sons set sail from Bristol in the *Matthew* in 1497. The tower is 105 ft. high and there are 109 steps to the top. It is surmounted by the winged figure of Commerce holding a boat.

137.   Clifton Zoological Gardens consists of 12 acres of land, acquired in 1835 from Francis Adams. The leading spirit was Dr. Henry Riley, a physician at the Royal Infirmary. Adjacent to the zoo were 15½ acres of pasture, bought in 1860-1 to found a public school. The first buildings of Clifton College were opened in September 1862, and they are pictured *c.*1920.

138.   The first buildings of Clifton College were designed by Charles F. Hansom and stone for their constructon was brought from Bath. The chapel, with its detached spire, was completed in 1866, and various buildings in the Gothic style were added up to the 1920s. The school served as General Omar Bradley's headquarters during the Second World War.

139. The Clifton Rocks Railway was built by Sir George Newnes, together with the hydropathic institution and pump room, which opened as the Clifton Grand Spa Hydro in 1898. The tunnel is 500 ft. long at a gradient of more than 1 in 2, and the railway was fitted with more than four pairs of rails. It represents the final effort to re-establish the Hotwell Spa at the end of the 19th century, but closed in 1934.

140. The Rocks Railway was acquired by the Bristol Tramways and Carriage Co. on 29 November 1912 for £1,500, and was closed in 1934. This is the only known view of all four of the 18-seat cars together, and shows the track and cars being dismantled.

OFF FOR THEIR ANNUAL OUTING 10.

141.   George Müller, born in Prussia in 1805, came to England aged 24 to study. He became minister of an Independent Church, and came to Bristol in 1836. Muller founded an orphanage at Ashley Down which housed 300 children, but as demand increased so did his buildings until 2,050 children were accommodated. By 1886, 7,294 were being cared for, although Müller had retired in 1872.

142.   The first horse-drawn tram started on 9 August 1875 from Upper Maudlin Street, via Queens Road and Whiteladies Road to the foot of Blackboy Hill. The top-hatted figure on the step of the tram is Sir George White (1854-1916). He was the secretary, later chairman, of the Bristol Transport and Carriage Company, and subsequent founder of the Bristol Aeroplane Company.

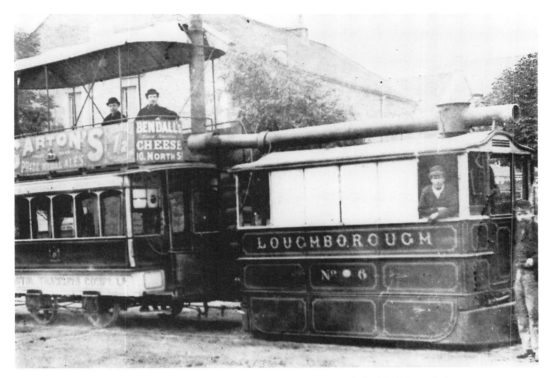

143. The first effort to mechanise the horse-drawn trams was made in 1880-1, and there was a 12-month trial period on the Horfield route. For the first time the tram, which had become a trailer, had a canopy to save passengers from the exhaust fumes. The first trams had room for 16 passengers inside and 20 outside. The Tramways Company reverted to horses after a year.

144. In 1894 a provisional order was obtained to convert the four mile Old Market to Kingswood line to electric traction. The Power House was built alongside the depot at St George, and an electric service began on 14 October 1895. The Tramways Co. then bought Finzell's Sugar Warehouse at Counterslip and converted it into a generating station. Here an electric train is drawing a horse tram in 1896.

145.   Bristol's first motor bus is seen here on 17 January 1906, its first day on a route from the Suspension Bridge along Merchant's Road and Victoria Square to the Victoria Rooms. It is turning into Merchant's Road outside the department stores of Cordeux and Sons which opened in 1863. The buses ran every ten minutes during the day and every 15 minutes in the evening.

146.   The big raid of 24 November 1940 did not receive the publicity which other towns like Coventry had been given.
Bristol had suffered 1,159 deaths from enemy action up to this time, less than Birmingham or Liverpool, but the sixth
highest in the country. On 24 November 30 shops were totally destroyed in Park Street, six were burnt out, and three were
seriously damaged.

147. The same raid saw the destruction of the University Great Hall and its glorious hammer-beam roof, one of the finest in England. The Hall was in use as the library for King's College, London, and contained many thousands of volumes brought down from London for their students. The Wills family immediately set aside seasoned oak to rebuild the Hall.

148. Park Street and the University are shown here after the November 1940 raid. On 11 April 1941 bombs fell on the old Coliseum in Park Row next to the University Library which adjoined it. This was the last of the major raids on the city. There had been 548 alerts and 77 occasions when bombs had fallen, killing 1,299 people.

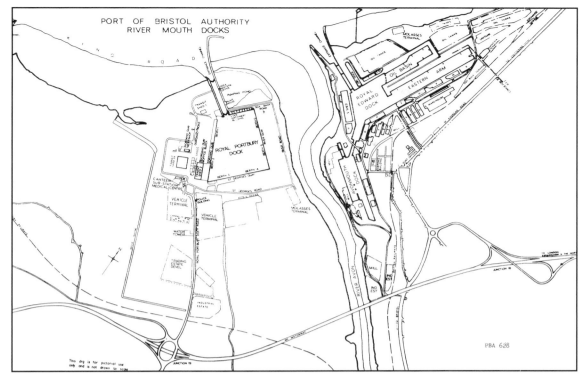

149.   Avonmouth Dock opened in 1877, the Royal Edward Dock (by King Edward) in 1908, and the eastern extension was opened in May 1930 by the Prince of Wales. In 1927 nearly one million tons of grain imports were received at Avonmouth, 10 per cent of the British total. There was a large trade in flour and meal, oilseeds, bananas, fruit, sugar, petroleum, zinc concentrates, tobacco and wood.

150.   Avonmouth Old Dock and Channel into the Royal Edward Dock, March 1921. The Channel is 75 ft. wide. General cargo berths are equipped with cranes the capacity of which ranges from three to ten tons. West Wharf is used for the discharge of West African cargoes of cocoa and timber. It is also used for the discharge of fertilisers, animal feedstuffs and coal.

151. Avonmouth Docks, 1930. The photograph shows the entrance lock to the Royal Edward Dock, the Dry Dock, the Oil Basin and, on the further side, the Eastern Arm providing six extra berths. Water depths within the Royal Edward Dock and Avonmouth Old Dock range from 25-36 ft., the majority of berths offering 32 ft. or more.

152. Prior to sailing, the ships moved to the passenger terminal at the Royal Edward entrance lock, built in 1910, and seen here in 1923. A special boat train was assembled at Temple Meads. The station was chiefly used for the West Indies by Elders and Fyffes' Line, Henderson and Bibby Lines from Rangoon, and the Federal Line from Australia and New Zealand.

153. Bulk grain being bushelled into sacks, 1910. In 1910 there were two granaries, the Co-operative Wholesale Society Granary and the Royal Edward Dock Granary. Four hundred tons an hour could be discharged into the silo granary which could store 10,000 tons. The C.W.S. mill was steam driven and served by the Pensford and Bromley Colliery in the North Somerset coalfield.

154.   Discharging oil at the Royal Edward Dock Oil Jetty, in 1920. The Royal Edward Dock has a self-contained oil basin equipped with common-user pipeline facilities for private and public tankage. British Petroleum took over the Western Petroleum Company in 1908 and by 1911 imported 118,000 tons into Avonmouth from Rumania and Mexico.

155.   Discharging bananas at 'N' berth, Avonmouth in 1930. Hundreds of dockers are moving stems of bananas upon their shoulders into railway trucks. Fyffes used coal-fired ships, and carried 100 passengers in two- and three-berth cabins on the main and promenade decks. In 1938 a Jamaica round trip was £42 (£27 in the 'B' class).

156.   Excavating clay from the Patchway Tunnel for Brunel's line to the Severn estuary, Charles Richardson, Brunel's resident engineer, realised it was hard and excellent for brickmaking. He bought Cattybrook Farm, near Almondsbury, and began making bricks from 1864. By 1900 Cattybrook Brickworks (seen here *c.*1910) had 21 kilns and made 20 million bricks a year. It is now Ibstock Building Products Ltd.

157.   National Smelting Works, Avonmouth in the 1920s. Before 1914 Australia sent much of its zinc concentrates to Germany for refining, while Britain imported from Germany most of the refined zinc needed. When war began the Government initiated the setting-up of the National Smelting Company and sulphuric works at Avonmouth between 1917 and 1923. The company was taken over in 1929 by the Imperial Smelting Corporation.

158.   George White, chairman of the Bristol Tramways Company, switched some of his tramway workers at Filton to aviation work in 1910 and, by November, 14 Boxkites had been made. During the year Maurice Tetard, the famous French aviator, flew at 100 ft., circled, and landed again in front of thousands on the Downs.

159.   Three Bristol Boxkites outside their hangars at Sir George White's British and Colonial Aeroplane Company, Filton, in 1910. Seventy-eight Boxkites were built, 43 for military use. The standard Boxkite pusher biplane had a maximum speed of 45 mph. from a 50hp. Gnome engine. Boxkites were exported to Australia, Russia, India, Spain and France.

160.   When war broke out in August 1914 all civil flying was banned and Filton built Government-designed and financed B.E. biplanes which began production in 1912. There were 400 employees at Filton and they produced a plane a day. By 1915 the B.E.2 variants in service (an example shown here c.1915) were due for replacement, and Filton went on to design the Scout and Bristol Fighter biplanes.

161. Bristol Waggon and Carriage Works was founded in 1851 in Temple Street by John Fowler, inventor of the steam plough, and Albert Fry. It continued until 1866 under Albert Fry and his cousin, Theodore, but Albert moved the firm to Lawrence Hill. There were two distinct departments: railway stock and road vehicles. This is the painting shop in 1906.

162.   The Beaufighter (photographed at Filton in the 1940s) was a descendant of the famous Blenheim, of which 5,000 were built at Bristol. The Beaufighter was powered with two 1,400hp. 14-cylinder radial Bristol Hercules engines and became the R.A.F.'s favourite night fighter when fitted with airborne interception radar.

163. The clocktower building at William Champion's Warmley Brass Works, built after 1761. An inventory of 1761 included 22 copper furnaces, 15 brass furnaces, three rolling mills, five water battery mills with 12 hammers and one spelter works with five furnaces. Other brass companies existed at St Philips, Crew's Hole, and at Conham, near Crew's Hole.

164. The Great Western Cotton Factory was sited beside the Feeder Canal in Barton Hill, and opened in 1838. Over 1,500 workers were employed and five of the seven directors were from northern towns. It survived for a century but in 1925, hit by recession, it went into liquidation. From 1929-68 it was used as a warehouse, and then demolished.

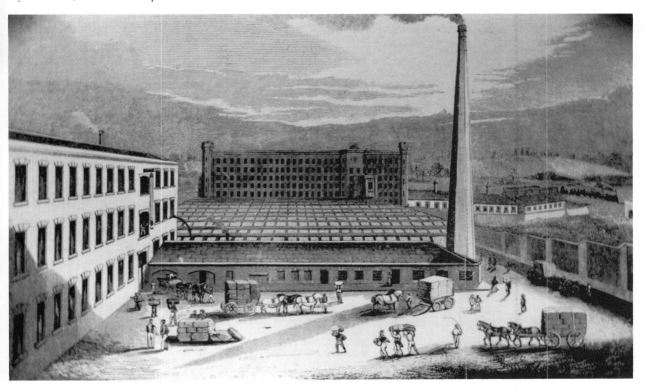

165. Butler's Tar Distilling Works, Crew's Hole, St George. William Butler came to Bristol in 1843 to manage Roberts and Daines' new works at Crew's Hole. Following a fire in 1863 Roberts and Daines sold out to Butler. The company produced creosote, pitch, napthalene, benzole, aniline dyes, toluene and ammonia. In 1962 the firm moved to Avonmouth, producing antiseptics, preservatives and disinfectants, until taken over by an American company, Tenneco Organics.

166. Conrad Finzel's Sugar Refinery on the Counterslip. Finzel died on 21 October 1859. German by birth, he invented and patented improvements to sugar refining. For many years he gave between £3,000 and £10,000 to Müller's orphanages. In the 1860s the refinery was one of the largest in the country, but closed in April 1881 because the Disraeli Government would not countenance protective duties.